UNIONS IN AMERICAN NATIONAL POLITICS

UNIONS IN AMERICAN NATIONAL POLITICS

Graham K. Wilson

Lecturer in Government
University of Essex

St. Martin's Press   New York

ISBN 0-312-83305-9

Library of Congress Cataloging in Publication Data

Wilson, Graham K
    Unions in American national politics.

    Includes index.
    1. Trade-unions—United States—Political activity.
I. Title.
HD8076.W54 1979   322'.2'0973   79-15559
ISBN 0-312-83305-9

For my father, brother and family,
and Philip Williams

Contents

Preface

Trades unions are not a subject conducive to dispassionate study. For obvious reasons unions have become a *bête noire* for conservatives in both Britain and the United States. The existence and strength of unions rest on collective action rather than individual rights; unions (which still represent predominantly the working class) always seem on the verge of changing the distribution of income; and the reluctance of unions to submit to unfavourable legislation (be it an injunction to return to work under the Taft-Hartley Act in the USA or the Industrial Relations Act in Britain) can be construed as a challenge to the rule of law.

The attitude of the Left to unions is more complicated. Even European socialists with both intellectual and institutional ties to organised labour feel somewhat ambivalent about unions which, they think, are all too often vehicles of narrow self interest rather than idealism or, as in the famous cartoon image of the British TUC as a cart horse, embody the unthinking, conservative aspects of the working class. Marxists tend to be even more disparaging about unions. Support for trades unions is but a paltry step for the workers in the formation of class consciousness; as Lenin noted the working class on its own is capable of *mere* trades union consciousness (emphasis added). Unions are often accused from the Left of class collaboration, of betraying the long term interests of their members by short term compromises. American radicals, less influenced than the European Left by the Marxist tradition of seeing the working class as the means for transforming society, are even more sceptical about unions. Indeed, unions are often seen not as a potential source of aid to disadvantaged groups but as a barrier to their progress through their alleged complicity in discriminatory labour practices.

In some ways, unions encourage the application of unusually high standards to themselves. Ringing phrases that the labour movement is a crusade or it is nothing are heard frequently in Britain where even union constitutions contain commitments to seeking the socialist society. Similar paper commitments to a long term ideal (even if not always socialism) can be found amongst European and American unions, too. In writing this study I have avoided any preconceptions about what the role of unions in society ought to be. This is partly because I do not find class theories a useful approach to the study of unions or labour movements, which seem to me to display an enormous diversity. As Walter Kendall has demonstrated in his study *The Labour Movement in Europe*, history, politics, economics and social forces combine to create a different union movement from country to country, even within Western Europe. Too many discussions of American unions and politics seem to me to start with a model of what the authors take to be a model of normal union development and then proceed to explain the American departure from it. The model of union development used is usually one in which unions, eager to promote the development of socialism, form a class-conscious political party to further their ideals. Such a model seems to me to fit remarkably few countries, even in Europe, and little is to be gained, therefore, by starting with the assumption that American unions *should* fit that model.

Another reason why I have tried to avoid any preconceptions about the form that the political involvement of unions should take is that I have long suspected that much ignorance and confusion surrounds a much simpler question; namely, what the nature of the relationship between unions and politics is, particularly in the USA. Why this question has been so little researched is something of a mystery to me. Perhaps it is the case that because so many people have strong views on what they think the relationship between unions and politics ought to be, they assume that they know already what that relationship is in practice. I suspect, and indeed hope, that many people do not know what the relationship between unions and politics is in the USA, and will be somewhat surprised by the conclusions which I reach. I suspect, too, that my findings will be interpreted in different ways by radicals and conservatives. Radicals will be struck by the unadventurous goals which American labour has sought, while conservatives will stress that unions have been playing politics instead of advancing their members' interests. I hope that I shall at least provide some fresh evidence for both sides.

I wish to express my thanks to the many senators, congressmen, and officials of the Department of Labor, American Federation of Labor-Congress of Industrial Organizations, (AFL-CIO), Teamsters, United Auto Workers and other unions who gave me their time and patience. A very special word of thanks is due to Evelyn Dubrow of the International Ladies Garment Workers' Union who did much to help me arrange interviews. I should add that none of the people interviewed or who helped in any way can be held responsible for any of the errors of fact or opinion which may exist in this book. The Brookings Institution provided me with an ideal base from which to work; Mrs Joanne Kirchner typed the manuscript with great care and skill; Mr Harry Goldstein, Mr David Robertson and Mr Philip Williams provided useful comments, again without being responsible for any surviving mistakes. Finally, none of the research on which this study is based would have been possible had it not been for the generosity of the Nuffield Foundation in funding my research. I hope it will not seem a major departure from objectivity if I say that one of the joys of working on this project has been meeting so many pleasant people.

University of Essex   Graham K. Wilson
August 1978

Some Common Abbreviations

AFL-CIO	American Federation of Labor-Congress of Industrial Organizations
AFSCME	American Federation of State, County and Municipal Employees
COPE	Committee on Political Education (of the AFL-CIO)
ILGWU	International Ladies Garment Workers' Union
UAW	United Auto Workers
UMW	United Mine Workers of America

1 American Labour Today

American unions enjoy a mixed reputation and little popularity. Conservatives within the United States view unions as an undesirable force which disrupts the smooth functioning of a market economy and, to make matters worse, mobilises resources to help liberal politicians. American liberals, on the other hand, increasingly tend to regard unions as just another 'special interest' group, which is oblivious to the problems of the poorest in America and hostile to liberal attitudes on issues of personal morality such as sex or the use of non-addictive drugs. Trades unionists outside the United States also tend to be sceptical. American unions are not nearly as successful as those of Britain, Austria, Germany, the Low Countries or Scandinavia in recruiting members. Moreover, even more than American liberals, European union activists tend to be dismissive about the political role of American unions because they have not been Marxist or even overtly social democratic.

Many of the left-wing critics of American unions start from either the assumption that unions abroad are much more political and 'progressive' than American unions or that American unions were once much more left-wing or 'liberal' than they are now. In fact comparisons made with European unions tend to be highly selective. After all, neither German nor Swedish unions are radical critics of the social system these days. In both countries the unions accept the capitalist system and seek specific reforms within it. In Italy and France major portions of the union movement were created by the Christian Democrats in order to forestall socialism and communism; their political role has been to support conservative political parties.[1]

Even Britain, often assumed to be the extreme case of a politically active, socialist labour movement, is not as simple an example as it would appear to be at first sight. Few British union leaders use their union's money or organisation to further political goals which do not affect their members directly. Each of the three pillars of the British labour movement (the co-operative movement, the unions and the political party) used to be assumed by members of the Labour Party to

TABLE 1.1:   *Union Membership as a Proportion of Workforce 1932–72*

Year	Total union membership excluding Canada	Membership as % of total workforce	Non-agricultural workforce
1932	3,050,000	6.0	12.9
1942	10,380,000	17.2	25.9
1952	15,892,000	24.2	32.5
1962	16,586,000	22.6	29.8
1972	19,435,000	21.8	26.7

Source: US Department of Labor, *Handbook of Labor Statistics, 1975* – Reference Edition, Government Printing Office, Washington DC, 1975.

TABLE 1.2:   *Trade Union Density in the United States, Britain and the EEC*

	No. of wage and salary earners in unions	Union members as % of non-agricultural workforce
United States[a]	19,435,000	26.7
Federal German Republic[b]	7,900,000	37.0
France	3,050,000	20.0
Italy	7,000,000	57.0
Netherlands	1,520,000	42.0
Belgium	1,856,000	66.0
Luxembourg	50,000	50.0
United Kingdom	10,674,000	46.0
Ireland	386,000	50.0

Source: (a) as Table 1.1
(b) Coventry and District Engineering Employers' Association, *Labour Relations and Employment Conditions in the European Economic Community*, Coventry, 1972, p. 30; from the Statistical Office of the European Community figures.

be best left to handle their areas of responsibility without interference. Party leaders did not tell union leaders how to pursue wage claims, and union leaders did not interfere with Parliamentary tactics. Only in emergencies or on crucial issues such as rearmament in the 1930s, unilateral disarmament or the maintenance of a purely theoretical commitment to the nationalisation of the means of production, distribution and exchange embodied in Clause IV of the Party's Constitution did union leaders play a conspicuous political role. From 1941, when Labour entered the wartime coalition, to the fortuitous advent of Frank Cousins to the leadership of the Transport and General

Workers' Union, the political role of British unions was largely to help the Parliamentary leader defeat the ultra-left.[2] Since the advent of Cousins, British unions have been distributed over the spectrum of Labour Party opinion with one of the giants, the TGWU on the left and another, the General and Municipal Workers' Union (GMW), on the right. The much discussed politicisation of the Trades Union Council probably has resulted not so much from a rediscovery or discovery of the joys of political action by unions as from the increasing preoccupation since 1960 of both Labour and Conservative governments with the details of industrial relations and wage settlements. British unions have been pulled into politics by the politicians.[3]

Just as the political commitment of European unions is overestimated, so too is the degree to which unions in the USA were once thought, but have since ceased, to be a radical political force. According to legend, American unions, particularly the new mass production unions in the steel, auto and rubber industries, were real forces for social change before the last war but have since been 'co-opted' into accepting the existing social order. The reality is far different, however. Unions were not a *force for* radical politics in the 1930s; they were the *objects of* sympathy and support from radicals and liberals. In the face of determined, often violent, opposition from employers and the Great Depression, unions were too concerned with the problems of organising and securing good pay settlements to participate in politics, even though CIO organisers frequently had strong political beliefs. In spite of Roosevelt's famous order to 'clear it with Sidney' – i.e., consult Sidney Hillman, head of the CIO, on the Vice Presidential nomination of 1944 – unions played a puny part in American politics until the 1950s. Indeed, the supposedly radical unions grouped in the Congress of Industrial Organizations (CIO), created by a Republican, John L. Lewis, came close to disbanding their small Political Action Committee (PAC) after the Second World War.[4] This is not to argue that radical beliefs or sentiments in the CIO were rare, but merely that political action had a low priority. If there is any steady trend, it is for American unions to be more widely and intensely involved in politics than ever before. There was no Golden Age of radical unionism in America's past.

What, however, are the genuine historical traditions of American unionism which affect the movement today? In fact, there are several conflicting traditions which leave their mark. American labour has rarely been united. In the 1930s the new mass unions formed with the help of the CIO found it impossible to stay in the American Federation of Labor (AFL). Though the AFL and CIO merged in 1955, the merger did not, as we shall see, end their differences, and in 1967, the United Auto Workers (UAW) allowed their membership of the AFL-CIO to lapse. In spite of occasional rumours that the UAW will re-affiliate, this appears unlikely during the lifetime of the present President of the AFL-CIO, George Meany. (Indeed, in October 1977 the UAW confirmed its decision to stay out.) The Teamsters Union, the largest single union in the United States, was expelled for corruption in 1957. As the National Educational Association which increasingly functions as a school teachers' union, is also not affiliated, the three largest unions in the USA remain outside the AFL-CIO.

Although both personality clashes and national politics have divided the American labour movement, it is undeniable that the major division has been between craft and business unionism on the one hand, and its opponents in the industrial unions on the other.

Samuel Gompers achieved the formation of the first permanent federation of trade unions in the United States. Gompers is remembered for his negative attitudes such as his opposition to partisan activity by labour, his rejection of social security and health policies controlled by the State and narrow vision of labour's goals (which he defined as 'more'). It is tempting to conclude from this that Gompers was an early Archie Bunker (the American counterpart to Alf Garnett) exhibiting the crass prejudices of the American worker. Such a conclusion would be incorrect. Gompers was a sophisticated thinker versed in Marxist rhetoric. (His argument against proposals that health and social security benefits should be provided by the State rested ultimately on the proposition borrowed from the *Communist Manifesto* that the State is the executive arm of the bourgeoisie.)[5] Gompers' opposition to an extensive political role for labour was clearly justified by the twin dangers of unpopularity if labour politics were dominated by fringe socialist groups whose appeal would be (like that of Debs) primarily to recently arrived immigrants, and on the other hand, the risk of splits incompatible with unionism if labour politics were dominated by the religious and regional loyalties which dominated American politics until the Second World War. Although Gompers, like AFL Presidents after him, may have stayed too long for the good of his own reputation or the AFL, his approach was almost certainly necessary to establish unions in the United States of the late nineteenth century.

Nonetheless, Gompersism was interpreted by the aged Gompers himself and the lesser men who followed in a stultifying way. The AFL, which like the 'new model' trade unionists in Britain in the late nineteenth century based its success on avoiding political controversy and appealing to the skilled worker, became actively hostile to the organising of the less skilled. Yet, as John L. Lewis, President of the United Mine Workers (UMW) knew only too well from experience, the existence of a large body of unskilled workers on the fringes of the unionised sector of American industry weakened the industrial power of the unions within the AFL. Large pay claims increased the incentive for mining companies to recruit non-union labour. The craft unions became, like medieval guilds, organisations to restrict the supply of skilled labour, acting through hiring halls as surrogate employers and sharing with American society ugly racial prejudices in dealing with applications for apprenticeships. There is an interesting revisionist argument made by Louis S. Reed that during much of Gompers's Presidency the AFL Executive was more receptive to measures such as compulsory social insurance and old age pensions than Gompers himself. Reed also argues that 'Gompers's and the Federation's interest and activity in matters political . . . was a constantly rising curve'.[6] However, it would seem perverse to deny that had the AFL continued to control the development of American unions, they would have re-mained organisations representing a tiny minority of the workforce – this minority being by and large the most skilled, with little interest in politics except to serve their narrowest interests.

In the 1930s, however, developments slipped out of the control of the AFL. John L. Lewis, whose union faced a continuing problem with competition from the unorganised, was determined to launch a major drive to increase the proportion of the workforce unionised. Faced with indifference and even hostility from the AFL, Lewis's Committee for Industrial Organizations transformed itself into an independent Con-gress of Industrial Organizations. It is worth reiterating that the CIO was a beneficiary rather than a creator of liberal support. Liberal congressmen and senators – elected before mass unions existed which could help them win elections – adopted vital legislation outlawing the issuing of court injunctions to end strikes and, most importantly of all, passed the Wagner Act. The Wagner Act did much to make employers accept unions for the less skilled worker. Apart from establishing in law the right to join a union, it prohibited 'unfair' tactics by employers designed to discourage workers joining unions, and, above all, created a federal agency, the National Labor Relations Board, which would conduct fair secret ballots in which workers could vote in favour of having a union. The refusal of state and federal authorities to follow their common practice of bloodily suppressing strikes, and their willingness to tolerate the 'sit-ins', which were of doubtful legality but were vital to the success of unions in the struggles to organise the steel and auto industries, was crucial too.

The unions which emerged in the 1930s were very different from the bulk of those in the AFL. They represented not crafts or skills but industries. Both carpenters and assembly line workers for Fords could, at least in theory, join the United Auto Workers. As the new unions were predominantly located in the new mass production industries, such as cars and rubber, the bulk of their members tended to be unskilled. Though not the worst off in the United States, their members were decidedly not as prosperous as the skilled craftsmen organised by the AFL. Ironically, the industrial unskilled worker whom Gompers had feared would be used to depress the earnings of the skilled worker had been organised into unions with a militant image.

The CIO unions devoted little attention to politics in the 1930s. Radical rhetoric was not translated into political action. Indeed, John L. Lewis reverted to his allegiance to the Republican Party in 1940 when he vainly tried to throw the votes of the CIO's members to the Republican candidate, Wendell Willkie. Yet the importance of the Wagner Act and restrained reaction to the sit-ins by the authorities necessarily made the CIO unions much more sensitive to the importance of politics than most AFL unions. This difference should not be overdrawn into a picture in which the CIO, as a mirror image of the AFL, was a politically radical, active and class-conscious movement. In fact, the CIO's political activity was on a small scale and uncertain. Some of the unions which reverted to the AFL, such as the International Ladies Garment Workers' Union (ILGWU), were equally as politically aware. On balance, however, the CIO unions did contain more activists, such as the Reuther brothers who thought of the union movement partly as a more important base for progressive politics than the AFL unions. Indeed, members of CIO unions, who were less affluent than craft workers, made up a natural constituency for liberal politicians. In these crucial years, immediately after the end of the Second World War, the CIO unions were both a source of support and a battleground for those politicians who, grouped around the Americans for Democratic Action (ADA) were working to establish a progressive but anti-communist force firmly committed to the Democratic Party.[7] If the stereotype AFL union is a selfish, introspective craft union, the stereotype of a CIO union is of a more militant union composed predominantly of unskilled workers whose leader is committed to numerous liberal causes. Yet American labour would not have played the role it has in federal politics if these stereotypes had remained quite so distinct.

THE MERGER OF THE AFL AND CIO

The balance of power between the AFL and CIO at the time of their merger in 1955[8] can be appreciated only in the light of the way in which the CIO had lost impetus, and the AFL revived. The AFL remained the larger grouping of unions. It had recruited many more new members during the Second World War than had the CIO. Indeed, the CIO was stagnating. John L. Lewis had led the United Mine Workers out of the CIO shortly after he had been obliged to resign its Presidency as a consequence of CIO members conspicuously rejecting his advice to vote for Willkie rather than Roosevelt in 1940. Eleven unions were expelled from the CIO in the 1940s because they were said to be controlled by communists. Finally, the CIO's prestige was severely threatened by the rumoured withdrawal of the United Steelworkers, its second largest union, and its plans to affiliate to the AFL. It was the AFL, not the CIO, which entered the merger talks from a position of strength. Between 1939 and 1953, the AFL's share of union membership had risen from 62 per cent to 64 per cent, while the CIO's fell from 23 per cent to 20 per cent.[9]

The AFL, too, had suffered a shock, however. Though the AFL, in contrast to the CIO, had not been the initial beneficiary of the labour legislation of the 1930s (though its wartime expansion was aided by the laws), it had assumed that legislation damaging to unions was highly unlikely. Just how far the truth of this assumption was dependent on the maintenance of a Democratic majority in Congress was illustrated by the passage in 1947 of the Taft-Hartley Act by a Republican-majority Congress. We shall discuss the provisions of this Act in a later chapter. Suffice to say here that the Act shifted the balance of power in favour of management. Further expansion by the unions was made difficult and union officials were even fearful for the prospects of existing unions. Many union leaders feared that the 'cooling off' period would make successful strike action all but impossible. The prohibition of the closed shop would lead to mass resignations by members eager to save their dues. Such fears were misplaced but acute. The Taft-Hartley Act was passed over the veto of President Truman, which is to say that it attracted the support of over two-thirds of congressmen and senators. This in itself seemed to demonstrate that American labour was politically weak and vulnerable. The AFL comforted itself with the thought that congressmen who had supported the Act would meet their doom at the next election. When this proved not to be the case, the assumption that AFL unions could afford to ignore politics was shattered. Unions might ignore politics, but politicians would not ignore them. The AFL unions rapidly created the Labour League for Political Education, first in some states—California[10] for one—and subsequently nationally.

This tendency for the AFL to be extensively involved in politics was powerfully strengthened by the accession of George Meany to the Presidency of the AFL. Meany's first major post in the AFL had been as a lobbyist for it in New York State politics. Raskin notes that Meany was a product of the 'emphasis on legislation and lobbying brought by the New Deal' and 'started with the thesis that labour had to be heavily involved in politics to safeguard the gains it made at the bargaining table, or to win them in the first place'.[11] Meany's own view was that it was impossible to influence legislation satisfactorily by lobbying alone. As Meany put it: 'How do you get legislation and stay out of politics and refrain from political action?'[12] Thus, by the time that the merger with the CIO occurred, the AFL had gone far to disprove the accusation that it was indifferent to politics. Douty, a leading commentator, noted on the eve of the merger of the AFL and CIO that 'While the Federation plainly has not lost faith in the value of collective bargaining for improving the workers' lot, it has elevated government and politics to something approaching an equal role.'[13]

To what degree, then, did the different traditions of the AFL and CIO survive within the AFL-CIO after the merger of 1955? Clearly, the CIO's leaders were faced with the unwelcome fact that the sort of unionism they believed in had reached its peak. On the other hand, Taft-Hartley forced the AFL to recognise that the CIO's interest in politics had been probably too small, not too great. Yet, though there had been a considerable convergence, crucial issues remained unanswered. One of these was to what extent American unions would involve themselves in politics. Clearly legislation damaging to the industrial activities of unions such as the Taft-Hartley Act would be opposed. It was uncertain whether the AFL-CIO would campaign, as Walter Reuther, President of the CIO, wished, for broad social and economic reforms, however. The affiliated craft unions were still inclined to prefer that the organisation confine itself to narrow labour issues. Some argued that broad political involvement would offend politicians whose sympathy could be gained on labour issues alone. Others contended that broad political issues such as the state of the economy and the level of employment determined the success with which unions could recruit members or secure wage increases. The AFL unions found a wider role harder to accept than the CIO unions.

Another unresolved question was the form which political involvement would take. Here again there were numerous possibilities. Unions could ally themselves with one of the established parties (in practice the Democrats), or they could form a new labour party. Unions could concentrate on skilful presentations of their case to legislators (i.e. through a *lobby*), an approach favoured by AFL unions, or they could intervene in elections hoping to change the composition of Congress and influence which party held the Presidency through the use of their members' votes and political contributions, an approach which found favour mainly in the CIO. Within the CIO, opinion had swung against any attempt to create a new labour party; after all, the limited success of the CIO itself suggested that the potential appeal of such a party was small. This did not imply that the AFL-CIO should commit itself to the Democratic Party. Meany and the AFL unions, following Gompers' enigmatic dictum that labour should punish its enemies and reward its friends, argued that the new organisation must preserve its freedom of action. The CIO unions were more ambivalent.

In short, the fact that in 1955 the AFL and CIO were agreed upon the need for political action did not mean that there was clear agreement on the form, extent or purpose of the AFL-CIO's involvement in politics. It would be premature to describe here the pattern that the political involvement of labour took; that is the purpose of the book as a whole. Our purpose here will be merely to outline how, and by whom, the key decisions were made about the political role of American labour.

THE BALANCE OF POWER INSIDE THE AFL-CIO

From the creation of the AFL-CIO in 1955 until the departure of the UAW in 1967 and the breach between Meany and the liberal unions in 1972, the key decisions about the involvement of labour in politics were made inside the AFL-CIO. Admittedly, the UAW always maintained a capacity for independent political action, but this was very much a sideshow until the union left the AFL-CIO. The distribution of power within the AFL-CIO and, in particular, who had the power to make the major decisions about labour's role in politics was crucial in deciding what political role labour would play.

In theory, the policy of the ALF-CIO is made by the biennial conference of the AFL-CIO and implemented under the guidance of the Executive Council elected at the conference. Officers, such as the President, were appointed by the conference. Yet there was widespread agreement that by the mid-1960s, the 27 members of the Executive Council who were not officers had ceased to exercise real power. Indeed, seven of them were no longer even presidents of unions; two had been defeated in elections and five had retired. Perhaps only a dozen members of the Executive exercised any influence. The rest, it is alleged, are ciphers who fill chairs and keep their mouths shut.[14]

Perhaps more important than this was that from the merger itself, the AFL unions dominated the AFL-CIO. This was symbolised by the fact that Meany of the AFL, not Reuther of the CIO, took the Presidency of the new body. Though this was explained by claims that Reuther readily conceded the post because, unlike Meany, he also had a major union to run, the reality was that the AFL took all the best posts because it was larger and, unlike the CIO, expanding. In 1953, the AFL's share of union membership was 64 per cent, while the CIO's was only 20 per cent. Perhaps not unreasonably, the AFL unions took seventeen of the seats on the Executive Council to the CIO's ten, a ratio which was expected to remain constant.[15] At lower but key levels, too, AFL men took the best jobs. Former AFL officials took over direction of the AFL-CIO's lobbying, political action and foreign policy units.

Reuther had clearly recognised the danger that the CIO would be swamped by the AFL and believed he had taken adequate precautions to prevent this. In the first place, the AFL-CIO would have an Industrial Union Department in which the CIO unions would congregate. In the second place, Reuther, much younger than Meany, expected to succeed him as President. Unfortunately for Reuther, the Industrial Union Department was never the CIO under another name. AFL unions rushed to join, diluting the CIO presence.[16] Meany, who had originally seen Reuther as his successor, grew to distrust and dislike him and determined not to cede him control.[17] Moreover, the CIO unions came to function less and less as a bloc. By 1961, Meany had settled nearly all demarcation disputes so that most of the CIO unions had had their grievances removed.[18] No longer were the CIO unions an aggrieved group constituting a reliable base for Reuther. Indeed, by 1965 there were only two regular Reuther supporters on the Executive Council.[19]

Reuther himself was not without blame for this situation. In spite of the qualities of courage and vision displayed during the struggle to create the United Auto Workers, Reuther lacked the temperament required for a long campaign against Meany within the AFL-CIO. Instead of discreet but determined plotting, Reuther neglected his allies, withdrawing for most of the time, first into the Industrial Union Department, then into the UAW itself, sallying forth to make unprepared and often inaccurate assaults on Meany. Disputes and personal rivalries continued at lower levels, too. Jay Lovestone, the backstage adviser to Meany on foreign policy, became a major irritant to the Reuther family. The Executive minutes also reveal disputes about how conscientiously old AFL staff served former CIO unions and the fairness of the financial settlement made at the merger. The disputes and rivalries often reduced the effectiveness of the AFL-CIO. Thus in 1962, the rivalry between Reuther and Meany over which of them should be part of Adlai Stevenson's delegation to the United Nations was so acute that the White House compromised by refusing to name either.[19]

In the end, blocked by the apparently indestructible Meany in his ambition[20] to become President and without significant support within the AFL-CIO, Reuther decided to leave. The final crisis exhibited all the features of poor preparation that had marred Reuther's time within the AFL-CIO. The break came over foreign policy. Reuther was slightly more doveish than Meany on Vietnam. That is to say Reuther believed that the United States should, without ending military involvement, try harder to negotiate with North Vietnam. Reuther was equally concerned about the close ties which had emerged between the AFL-CIO's services provided to help trades unions abroad and the activities of the Central Intelligence Agency. Foreign policy was the *casus belli*; as ever, there were other factors at work. Once the conflict had started, moreover, Reuther broadened the campaign. In late 1966 in a public speech, Reuther said that his differences with Meany on foreign policy were well known. However, he added, the issues were far broader. 'I disagreed because the labor movement under his [Meany's] leadership is failing in the broad social responsibilities it has to the total community of America.'[21] Reuther argued that the AFL-CIO was not giving adequate attention to issues such as civil rights and anti-poverty programmes which would benefit deprived Americans who were not members of unions. Unfortunately, some of Reuther's specific charges were false. For example, the AFL-CIO, contrary to Reuther's claims, had done far more to help Caesar Chavez organise the grape pickers than had the UAW. Even the gesture of leaving the AFL-CIO lost much force as Reuther had neglected to ensure that a single union would follow the UAW. Whatever one's sympathies for Reuther's goals, enhanced by his tragic death in an air crash soon after the UAW left the AFL-CIO, his tactics in pursuing them were not adroit, and Meany invariably out-maneouvred him.

Yet the power resources of a President of the AFL-CIO are not great. Like the General Secretary of the British TUC, the President of the

AFL-CIO plays no role in the negotiations conducted by individual unions. The powers of the AFL-CIO over individual unions are not great in theory; in practice, they are almost non-existent. Neither the Teamsters, expelled for corruption in 1957, nor the UAW, have suffered from being outside the AFL-CIO. Indeed, the Teamsters have increased their membership steadily since their expulsion. The AFL-CIO has succeeded in ending neither corruption nor racial discrimination in affiliates by threatening or using sanctions against them. Meany himself likes to claim that within broad limits, AFL-CIO allows great latitude to affiliated unions; it is a confederation. Leadership, Meany admits, exists but it is 'leadership by consent if you please'.[22]

How, then, did Meany consolidate his power? In the first place, Meany confined himself to issues like politics which, unlike wages, are not of major concern to union leaders. He also benefited from having natural ties to the building trades unions (as Meany was once a plumber) which are well represented on the AFL-CIO Executive. Twelve of the 31 Executive Council members are from craft unions. Meany has also benefited from the reluctance common in American unions to attack the leader who is a symbol of the movement as well as its officer. As Meany aged, the respect for age common in American unions also improved his position. So strong was this respect for the old man by 1972 that several members of the Executive voted, as Meany wished, not to support the Democratic candidate McGovern, yet subsequently committed their unions to work for him. Meany was prepared to add to these advantages by threatening to use the few sanctions available to him to enforce his will. In one row with Meany on the Executive Council in 1959, Reuther appeared to have the support of Joseph Carey, President of the Union of Electricians. Meany told Carey that if he sided with Reuther, a jurisdictional dispute between the electricians and competing unions would be decided to the electricians' disadvantage.[23] Carey saw sense. Meany, unlike Reuther, used his limited advantages adroitly. Whereas Reuther would launch an unprepared offensive, Meany would avoid bringing an issue to the Executive Council or Conference unless he was sure that he had the support he needed. As in Congress, such care creates an illusion of invincibility which, in time, itself becomes a powerful weapon. As his biographer, Goulden, puts it: 'Meany makes sure he has the votes before he puts an issue before the [Executive] Council.'

Yet Meany's power resources of prestige, skill and authority in jurisdictional disputes are not sufficient to guarantee success. For example, only with difficulty did Meany force the Michigan AFL and

CIO to merge at all.[24] At first, Meany was unable to impose settlements of competition for members. Thus competition between the UAW and construction unions for craftsmen within the auto industry continued throughout the 1950s.[25] However, on issues which are not vital to unions in industrial relations, of which political action is the clearest example, Meany enjoyed tremendous power. Meany does not try to determine the pay increases sought by individual unions such as the Steelworkers. In return, union Presidents usually allow Meany to take the lead on issues of less immediate concern such as political strategy.

Just as Meany is allowed a free hand by union presidents on many issues however, so Meany does not control all the day to day operations of the AFL-CIO's lobbyists or electoral campaigners. Yet partly because of the evidence about the struggle between Reuther and Meany from which the latter emerged victorious, we can be reasonably sure that the key men in charge of political action are not merely men in whom Meany has put his trust, but men who would appreciate the need to consult him before making key commitments.

THE STATE OF THE UNIONS

It is probably helpful to offer at this stage a brief picture of the American union movement. The most basic figures[26] to give are of membership. In 1972, there were nearly 19,435,000 union members in the United States. This amounted to 26.7 per cent of the non-agricultural work-force or 21.8 per cent of the total workforce. These figures are not high, and because of the recession of the mid-1970s which hit blue collar workers worse than managerial grades, the proportion organised has fallen off since. In general, however, the unions have halted the decline in membership which they suffered in the 1950s in terms of both the absolute size of unions and the proportion of the workforce belonging to unions; prior to the recession small scale growth had resumed. Between 1951 and 1968, 69 per cent of American unions grew by 10 per cent or more. However, this figure disguised the fact that a very large number of unions failed to grow or declined in membership. Because of both the differential growth of unions and amalgamations, the tendency has been for union membership to be concentrated in fewer unions. The largest 11 unions now account for over 47 per cent of union membership. One of the most important trends accounting for the halt in the decline of union membership in the United States had been the success of such public sector unions as the American Federation of State,

County and Municipal Employees (AFSCME). In fact, ten of the twenty-five fastest growing unions are in the public sector.

The fact that American unions represent only 26.7 per cent of the non-agricultural workforce is a political fact of much importance. Even more important, however, is the fact that trade union membership in the United States is geographically concentrated. Three states, New York, California and Pennsylvania, supply one in three American union members. These three states, plus Illinois, Ohio and Michigan, account for over half of the membership of American unions. That is not to say that they are the states with the highest percentage of the workforce unionised. In fact, the states with the highest union membership percentages are West Virginia, Washington and Pennsylvania. However, the concentration of union membership in relatively few states has major implications for American unions' political importance. There are large areas of the country where unions have few members, little organisation and, not surprisingly, little political strength.

The proportion of union membership in the AFL-CIO has fallen with the withdrawal of the United Auto Workers. At present, approximately 75 per cent of the total membership of unions belong to organisations affiliated to the AFL-CIO. The defection of the UAW has, however, produced a sharper fall in the number of states in which the AFL-CIO is absolutely dominant. There are now only 15 states in which over 80 per cent of total union membership is affiliated to the AFL-CIO; before the departure of the UAW, the figure was 36. Apart from the UAW, the major union outside the AFL-CIO is the Teamsters. The Teamsters Union, with nearly two million members, is not only the largest union, but also the fastest growing, representing workers such as lorry drivers whose cooperation is vital to the success of many other unions on strike; it is almost certainly corrupt. A third large union is the National Educational Association which, however, remains unsure whether it is a pressure group working to advance education or an organisation which bargains on behalf of teachers.

American unions in general have suffered from the reputation of the Teamsters. Unions in general are thought of as at best, oligarchic and at worst, corrupt. This is, in many ways, unfair to most unions. Most (61 per cent) of the unions in the AFL-CIO in 1969 had presidents elected after 1961, i.e. fewer than eight years before. Only 16.3 per cent of AFL-CIO unions had presidents elected 13 or more years before 1956. A recent study concluded that incumbents lost elections or failed to win promotion to a higher post much more frequently than is thought, and more frequently than in Britain.[27] Of course, not all union presidents who have held office for many years are corrupt, nor are all who win elections perfect. Examples from such major unions as AFSCME or the United Steel Workers serve to demonstrate that insurgent campaigns can displace established leaders with important consequences for the success and policy of the union.

In contrast, however, the United Mine Workers, before the victory of the reform candidate, Miller, had imposed 'trusteeships' or central control on 19 out of its 23 districts, thus suspending locally elected officials and meetings.

One final point is of interest. Though the American union movement has grown far beyond the craft unions, the craft unions retain a great deal of power within the AFL-CIO. Twelve of the 35 members of the Executive Council of the AFL-CIO are presidents of craft unions. As these unions are the most cohesive bloc in the Federation, their influence is considerable.

THE POLITICAL CHARACTER OF AMERICAN LABOUR

There is little doubt that from Meany downwards, the most powerful figures in the AFL-CIO have their roots in the AFL rather than the CIO. All this would lead us to suppose that the bulk of the American labour movement, the unions within the AFL-CIO with three quarters of unionised Americans, plays a limited political role. There is, after all, little doubt that the AFL was originally hostile to political action, defined the political interests of workers and unions narrowly, and represented primarily craft workers who have always been amongst the best paid sections of the workforce.

Our brief analysis of the balance of power within the AFL-CIO, confirming the importance of conservative craft unions, might seem to show the value of asking once more questions which are so often asked about American unions. Why are they apolitical? Why have unions not created a reformist movement such as the German, Scandinavian or British unions? Why are American unions perhaps not merely apolitical, but reactionary, supporting reactionary foreign policies?

Ingenious and profound explanation can be adduced to show why American labour, like American society, is different. The absence of a feudal legacy in the USA,[28] the dilution of class solidarity by ethnic rivalry and heterogenity, the comparative prosperity the United States has always enjoyed, or the obliteration of class consciousness by capitalist propaganda can be woven into intellectually stimulating combinations. Yet such theories beg a large number of important questions. Is it, in fact, true that American unions play a trivial role in politics? Is it true that their political involvement is focused on narrow, even selfish goals of benefit to unions or their members alone? How far is it the case that American unions have backed conservative causes?

The purpose of this book is to examine the evidence on these questions. This will be done by examining the involvement of unions in presidential and congressional elections, in lobbying and in the Democratic Party itself. We shall also see how the American system of industrial relations law impels unions into politics. The conventional wisdom about American unions on which many of the meta-theories about the uniqueness of American labour will be severely questioned; the image of selfish, reactionary, or apolitical American unions which both academics and even liberal activists in the United States accept will be rejected. Indeed, we shall conclude by raising questions about the ideology of liberals who have not merely accepted such images but have gone on to act on them, contributing at least as much as the unions to the absence of the links between unions and the democratic left, which observers take for granted in Britain.

2 Unions and Elections

Successful unions typically have a large number of members. One of the most obvious political advantages which this creates is the capacity to influence the outcome of elections. We have seen that American union leaders have long been aware of this possibility but were slow to develop the electoral potential of the union movement. Although Samuel Gompers had argued that unions should reward their friends and punish their enemies, little thought was given as to how they might do so until the passage of Taft-Hartley shocked both the AFL and CIO into creating machinery for intervening in election campaigns. When the AFL and CIO merged in 1955, the AFL's Labor League for Political Education and the CIO's Political Action Committee were merged into the Committee on Political Education, COPE. A number of questions remained to be answered, however. First, how extensive would be the commitment of the AFL-CIO to electoral action? The AFL had tended to place the emphasis of its limited political action on lobbying and electoral action was more associated with the CIO. Second, what sort of candidate would COPE back? The AFL tradition was one of concentrating on issues of immediate concern to unions and their members, whereas the expectation had developed (though there was little evidence to support this from the 1930s) that the CIO unions would involve themselves in broader political issues. How broad would COPE's political interests be? Finally, how effectively could unions, which are not of course primarily political, build a machine to intervene in elections?

THE SUPREMACY OF COPE

With significant very recent exceptions, to which we shall return at the end of this chapter, our focus will be primarily on COPE. This is not to dispute the fact that individual unions intervene in election campaigns. However, until the 1972 elections (the significance of which will be explained later), the bulk of electoral action was handled by COPE.

17

COPE had the best experts, the best machinery and the most information. Individual unions tended to give money to relatively small numbers of candidates, often at the behest of COPE, and lacked the machinery to intervene directly in election campaigns.

The view that COPE is pre-eminent has been challenged, however, by Irving Richter.[1] Richter notes that 'COPE's share of funds has gone down from roughly 38 per cent of total expenditures in 1958 to *less than 15 per cent in 1968.*' (Original emphasis).

TABLE 2.1:   *Expenditures on Elections by Unions and COPE*

Year	COPE $	TOTAL $ (including COPE)
1958	709,803	1,828,778
1964	941,947	3,816,242
1968	1,206,736	7,631,868

Richter interprets these figures as showing that COPE has declined steadily in importance. However, as Richter acknowledges, the expenditure figures are not a very satisfactory measure of labour's political activity. No allowance is made in them for the cost of voter registration drives, an activity on which COPE places great emphasis. Nor is allowance made in the figures for the fact that, as we shall see, COPE places more emphasis on providing services rather than funds to candidates. Moreover, it is legally permissible for unions to spend general funds on contacting their members during an election campaign to influence how they vote. It is not permissible for unions to make contributions to COPE from general funds. Finally, Richter does not allow for the fact that much of the money given to candidates by unions individually has been solicited through COPE. The author was able to attend a lunch organised by COPE in Washington for liberal Democrats from North Carolina at which they could solicit funds from the political directors of unions: COPE did not plan to give the majority of money itself but it did coordinate its dispersal. The main value of Richter's argument is not its devaluation of the role of COPE but its reminder of how significantly expenditures on elections by both COPE and unions individually have risen since the last war. The table shows that between 1958 and 1968, expenditure by COPE and individual unions rose by 317 per cent.

The Committee on Political Education is an organisation nominally separate from the AFL-CIO. Although its directors are the AFL-CIO's Executive and its staff at federal, state and local level use AFL-CIO buildings, this practice is necessary for legal reasons. Although federal law allows unions to use their general funds to communicate with members (even on political issues), general political activity is nominally supported by a voluntary levy only, as in Britain. However in 1977 the legal situation was complicated when the conservative Right to Work Committee (which is opposed to the closed shop) succeeded in obtaining a court order obliging the Federal Elections Commission (FEC) to bring an action against the COPE, alleging that it had been using federal funds on general political action. In particular, the FEC's suit contended that $392,000 from the AFL-CIO had been used since 1970 on political contributions, and that $600,000 had been transferred from the AFL-CIO's general account to COPE's 'Education Fund' in 1975 and 1976 alone.[2] The AFL-CIO has not challenged the detailed allegations but its Secretary Treasurer argued that the transfers 'represented a long-standing practice never previously challenged by federal auditors'.[3] Whether the courts will require the AFL-CIO to keep a greater distance from the COPE remains to be seen.

COPE is also large. Senator Fannin estimated that in 1968 labour unions distributed 118 million leaflets, provided 638 telephone banks, 24,611 people to man them and 72,225 canvassers.[4] Most of these efforts were made through COPE. The authoritative *Congressional Quarterly* estimated that labour spent $1 million on the 1974 mid-term elections.[5] In 1976, however, Senator Goldwater, who has many bones to pick with the unions, released estimates that unions spent $3,222,155 on Senate elections and $2,449,170 on House elections.[6] (The higher cost of Senate elections was probably due to the re-run of the New Hampshire Senate race after a dispute over who won the November race.) In the 1976 elections, COPE provided 120,000 volunteers, 20,000 telephones and used a computer bank listing 11,000,000 union members in 45 states to identify potential support for its candidates. The computer system was 'instrumental' in achieving 6,000,000 new registrations. Goldwater noted, however, that

It is quite important to observe that these figures do not include 'contributions in kind'. 'In kind' contributions include such things as manpower, mailing facilities and other expensive items of campaign work. The cost of these donations may run to nine or ten times the amount of the actual cash contributions.

The Right to Work Committee suit put election expenditure by COPE alone in 1976 at $3,000,000, most of it going to help the Carter–Mondale ticket.

Goldwater was wise to emphasise the importance of 'in kind' contributions. COPE itself does not dispense vast amounts of money. Its strength lies rather in the provision of 'in kind' services. Though COPE may well prompt the payments Fannin and Goldwater describe, COPE officials dislike making direct payments of great size. Indeed, they claim that the average COPE contribution to a Senate election campaign fund is only $10,000;[7] COPE prefers giving services to cash.

These services have become ever more sophisticated. Probably the most basic is the provision of organisers. One North Eastern Democratic representative interviewed reported that unions and COPE provided 138 paid officials to help in the latter stages of his campaign; this, too, in what is a safe district. Such organisers are often officials of the AFL-CIO or unions given paid 'leave' for all or part of the campaign. A second form of union support, and one which marks the increasing sophistication of COPE, is the identifying from union membership lists of potential supporters for endorsed candidates. COPE computers break down union membership lists first by congressional district, then by precinct, finally by street and block. Such lists can be used to recruit not only voters but volunteers for pro-labour candidates. Probably the most important service that COPE provides is before that stage, however, in getting union members registered to vote. Unskilled workers are less likely to register than those higher up the social ladder. Yet where COPE is strong, as in Pennsylvania, this trend has been overcome, and 80 per cent are registered. Similarly, Kornhauser *et.al.* [8] noted that the UAW, whose work in Michigan served as a prototype for COPE, was successful in registering a far higher percentage of its members than would have been expected for most blue-collar workers. A later study by Sheppard and Masters[9] concluded that the UAW registered over 90 per cent of its members and 87 per cent voted in the 1956 elections – a far higher percentage than their socio-economic status would have predicted. COPE at its best produces similar results.

Registration and 'get out the vote' drives do not stop with union members or even their families. It has long been traditional for labour organisations to work on entire districts rather than just on union members. Of late, this technique has been refined by employing specialists to register and organise ethnic minorities likely to support candidates whom COPE endorses. Thus both the UAW and AFL-CIO employ people whose task it is to turn out Hispanic Americans, blacks and even native Americans. The largest of these drives, aimed at raising the proportion of 'minority' Americans who register and vote, is rather nicely called 'Frontlash', in contrast to the feared 'backlash' of white voters. Another organisation, named after a famed black union leader, A. Philip Randolph, concentrates on mobilising blacks.

The scale of COPE activity has been rising. In 1958, a successful year for the candidates it endorsed, a business magazine reported that COPE had been involved in electing 221 members of the House.[10] In 1974, another good year for candidates it favoured, COPE offered help to 389 Representatives (of whom 270 won).[11] This has prompted many friends and foes to pay tribute to the efficiency of COPE. Its forceful director, Al Barkan, said in 1970:

> We're kind of proud of our organization. We've got organization in 50 damn states and it goes right down from the states to the cities. There's no party that can match us. Give us ten years or fifteen years and we'll have the best political organization in the history of this country.[12]

As political parties have been declining in strength as COPE grows, Barkan's remark has much force.

Yet there is another side to the picture. There are large parts of the United States, such as the South, where COPE has little strength, because unions have little strength. In the South labour unions and labour issues are unpopular. One liberal Congressman from North Carolina was heard by the author saying to a COPE official, 'I'd vote for repeal of 14(b) of Taft-Hartley if only you'd find a way to call it something else. Otherwise it's suicide.' COPE is not helpless in such areas. Funds can be channelled discreetly to favoured candidates, their arrival timed to avoid their revelation under the Campaign Finance Act until after the election. Organisers can be seconded, particularly those skilled in organising the black vote. But COPE's ability to operate as an open, active quasi-party is impaired very considerably. Even where COPE's support is not the kiss of death, however, all is not often perfect. One of the major problems COPE faces is simply staying in touch with its members. In a state such as Ohio, perhaps one-third of COPE affiliates change their address each year. Elsewhere its machinery may be imperfect. National COPE officials interviewed in private are less excited than Barkan about the quality of their organisation on the ground. Their doubts were confirmed by the unanimous preference amongst Congressmen interviewed for COPE's money rather than its organisational help. In some states, such as New York, COPE is well run and effective but preoccupied with state rather than national issues. COPE, in short, is a major force nationally, but its strength varies from state to state.

A state in which COPE is well organised but not omnipotent is Connecticut. Its activities are of some interest as a case in point. The Connecticut AFL-CIO had 168,000 members in 1974; 1.1 million people voted in the state that year. Union members and their families could make a major impact. When the state COPE checked its membership lists, however, it found that 25,000 of its members had failed to register. They were encouraged to do so. Local union officials were trained in how to register people, then given lists of the unregistered. By the end of September, the state COPE had switched from registering to persuading with two mailings going to each member's home encouraging him to vote for COPE-endorsed candidates. By late October, the effort had switched to 'getting out the vote'. Telephone banks were established in each labour district, and those manning them began contacting members to encourage them to vote for COPE-endorsed candidates. On election day itself, 300 volunteers checked off who had voted, so that after 6 p.m. the headquarters could begin contacting those who had failed to vote to try last-minute persuasion. The Connecticut COPE did very well in that over 90 per cent of its endorsees won in elections for the state legislature, and its nominees were also successful in the contests for Governor, Senate and four of the six contests for the House of Representatives. How far these successes were due to COPE's efforts is debatable. However, it did register between 15 and 20,000 union members who, with their families, were likely to support its nominees. On election day, 85 per cent of registered union members voted, compared with an average turnout in the state of 72.4 per cent. (Blue collar worker turnout could usually be expected to be below the average.) Total cash expenditure by the state COPE was $210,000, but its officials felt that their organisational efforts frequently provided winning margins.[13] They may well have been right.

THE STRUCTURE OF COPE

COPE is, on paper, a federation. The rules of COPE say that all endorsements of politicians except for President and Vice-President are in the hands of state and local bodies. The state COPE usually has the right to veto endorsements by local bodies. Endorsements for President and Vice-President of the United States are totally reserved to the national COPE taking its instructions from the AFL-CIO Executive.[14] These constitutional principles were put into effect in 1973. In the presidential election the previous year, the national AFL-CIO and COPE had decided to remain neutral. The Colorado COPE worked for the Democratic nominee, McGovern and, on being suspended, appealed to the AFL-CIO conference in 1973. It lost the appeal.[15] During the debate the rights of state AFL-CIOs and their COPEs were reaffirmed, but so too was the right of the national body to make all decisions on presidential endorsements. Paul Hall of the Seamen's Union, who led the case against the Colorado AFL-CIO, argued that had different branches of the AFL-CIO and COPE taken different positions on a presidential election, the power of the organisation would have been dealt a severe blow.

The rights of the national organisation in presidential elections are clear, therefore. But several other factors serve to weaken the autonomy of state and local bodies in other elections too. The first of these is finance. Though a state COPE can expect an automatic contribution of only $10,000 from national funds to work in a senate race, a national 'marginal' fund does exist to make extra donations to candidates who are involved in particularly close races or who are regarded as unusually deserving. On the other hand, state COPEs do usually provide the lion's share of labour's financial contributions; in Connecticut, whereas the average national contribution by COPE was $3,000, the state body gave between $5,000 and $15,000 to congressional candidates. A second nationalising factor is the influence of the national officials. Both the head of COPE (Al Barkan) and the AFL-CIO's chief lobbyist (Andrew Biemiller) are forceful personalities. Beyond this, however, local officials will often feel that the national officials are in a better position to evaluate someone (particularly if he is an incumbent) than they are. Those in Washington, it can be argued, know best how helpful an incumbent has been. If there is not an incumbent, however, so that the choice is between local politicians with no national record, the influence of the state and local COPE is likely to be greater.

By far the most important nationalising factor, however, is the existence of the COPE rating system. The COPE rating system selects a variety of issues (the selection of which is discussed below) and awards congressmen or senators a mark for each occasion they vote as COPE wishes. Thus 100 per cent indicates a perfect record; 0 per cent indicates the worst possible record. It is striking how often and easily the COPE record is used in discussions on which candidates to endorse. The author attended meetings to discuss which candidates for Congress should receive help from COPE and unions in the 1976 elections. Even when the state under discussion was in the South, the very first point made about any incumbent was his COPE record. As COPE ratings are determined nationally, this naturally strengthens the importance of the central part of the federal structure. Moreover, it would be gravely embarrassing if a congressman were endorsed at state level who had a poor COPE rating. Indeed, the national officials would bring every pressure to bear to prevent that happening.

We can imagine a variety of approaches COPE could follow in constructing its scale. The first would be to follow a narrow interpretation of Gompers' injunction to punish enemies and reward friends. This would involve campaigning against politicians on 'labour' issues such as the rights of construction unions to picket entire sites, not just one contractor (i.e. 'situs picketing'); abolition of section 14(b) of Taft-Hartley; abolition of the section of the Taft-Hartley Act empowering the President to order a 40-day 'cooling off' period; and the prevention of further anti-union legislation or appointments to bodies such as the National Labour Relations Board (NLRB) charged with its implementation.

A second strategy would add to such 'labour' issues matters which concern not only union members, but others too. A good example would be the management of the economy. Full employment benefits union members and makes securing large pay increases easier. Full employment also benefits minority groups such as blacks and Hispanic Americans and ghetto dwellers, all of whom suffer unusually high rates of unemployment. Another issue which could be included in this category is National Health Insurance. Third, and finally, unions might accept obligations to help those not in unions. In this way they would be not just institutions maximising benefits for their own members, but a labour movement concerned with social justice in general.

COPE publishes a booklet *How Your Senators and Congressmen Voted* for each session of Congress. The booklet contains a list of issues selected by the Committee and then grades legislators on them. Some picture of the balance of the issues taken into account by COPE appears below.

TABLE 2.2:   *COPE Issues – the House*

Year	Labour Issues	General	Regarding others
1961–2	2	7	2
1963–4	2	3	6
1965–6	3	2	5
1967–8	2	4	7
1969	2	6	4
1971	6	5	1
1972	4	5	2
1973	4	5	2
1974	4	6	1
1975	5	16	2
1976	6	15	2

The categories are based on the threefold distinction described above. A typical issue in column 1 would be repeal of Section 14(b) of Taft-Hartley that gives the states 'right to work laws' which ban closed shops. Issues in column 2 include medicare and public housing projects, benefiting both the poor and affecting construction wages respectively. Column 3 includes issues such as civil rights, rat control in ghettos and food stamps. (Very few, if any, members of American unions are poor enough to qualify as beneficiaries for the original food stamp programme.) Obviously, it is a matter of judgement where a particular issue belongs. The boundary is particularly difficult to draw between columns 2 and 3. For example, perhaps controversially, I have included votes on minimum wage laws in column 3 on the grounds that no American

TABLE 2.3:   *COPE Issues – Senate*

Year	Labour Issues	General	Regarding others
1961–2	1	8	2
1963–4	2	7	2
1965–6	3	3	5
1967–8	3	2	7
1970	2	6	5
1971	3	8	1
1972	4	3	3
1973	4	6	1
1974	7	3	1
1975	6	14	2
1976	4	16	0

union would accept a contract based on the minimum wage. The people whose wages are raised by minimum wage increases (unless they are put out of work) are the unorganised. It could be argued that minimum wage increases improve the prospects for union negotiators and the issue therefore belongs in column 2. My final defence would be that COPE officials do not see the issue that way but see it as benefiting others. The same exercise for the Senate yields similar results.

Clearly, the emphasis which COPE puts on the different sorts of issue varies and not all the reasons why this fluctuation occurs are under COPE's control. (Thus not every issue is voted on every year in Congress.) However, some generalisations which are perhaps surprising can be made. Most notably, COPE very rarely puts the emphasis on union issues; in only one year and in only one chamber (the Senate in 1974) did COPE base its evaluation of legislators primarily on how they voted on issues of immediate concern to unions and their members alone. In every other year, COPE's scale relied more heavily on issues of general importance (such as National Health Insurance or Medicare). On a few occasions (e.g. the Senate in 1967–8, the House in 1967–8 and 1963–4) the COPE scale was based mainly on issues which did not affect unions or many of their members directly at all (e.g. the Voting Rights Act) but instead benefited less privileged minorities in the USA. However, the tables do also show a tendency for the number of 'regarding others' issues to fall in the 1970s and the number of 'labour' issues to rise. The reasons for these trends are varied. Some reflect the ability of the Nixon and Ford Administrations to set the legislative agenda. Others reflect the unions' fears that for the first time in many years they faced a significant anti-union movement. By far the most important influence on the COPE ratings, however, have been the recessions of the 1970s, forcing it (along with groups such as the Black Caucus) to make unemployment the central issue prompting a large rise in 1975 and 1976 in issues coded as 'general'. Yet COPE remains unambiguously an organisation whose political concerns stretch far beyond the self interest of unions.

This is less surprising on reflection than one might suppose and can be explained in terms of the organisational self interest of the AFL-CIO. The AFL-CIO as such has little to do outside politics. Like most central bodies representing labour (e.g. the British TUC), the AFL-CIO can do little to affect wage negotiations or labour relations in a particular industry. The current President, George Meany, has been a strong 'centraliser' in terms of the traditions of the AFL. He has had limited success nonetheless. Drives against corruption failed embarrassingly in the 1950s when the members of the corrupt International Longshoremen's Association supported its New York leadership, and when the Teamsters, expelled for corruption, went from strength to strength. Similar constraints on the power of the AFL-CIO leadership have appeared in other areas. The Federation has failed to discover a way to prevent racism in constituent union locals; the United Auto Workers withdrew with impunity after a personality clash between its President, Walter Reuther, and Meany had been broadened into a disagreement over Vietnam.

One field left open to the leaders of the AFL-CIO, and where they have enjoyed considerable discretion, has been national politics. Issues affecting unions can often stir rivalries and antagonisms within the AFL-CIO too. In this sense, the safest ground for the AFL-CIO to occupy is that of national political issues. Unions which would not tolerate Meany interfering in their own affairs happily allow him to campaign for Medicare or National Health Insurance.

BENEFICIARIES OF COPE

It will come as little surprise that the AFL-CIO in its stand on general or 'regarding others' issues unambiguously takes what would be termed the 'liberal' position with one exception. That is to say, COPE approves of expanding the role of the federal government in controlling the economy, providing welfare services, protecting civil rights and liberties and in providing help for America's most deprived. The one area where the AFL-CIO's position is dubious is foreign policy. (Its strident criticism of authoritarian regimes such as that within the Soviet Union, causes many American liberals to call it conservative in foreign policy.) Quite predictably, therefore, COPE ratings are high for liberal congressmen or senators, who are usually Democrats, and low for conservative congressmen or senators, who are usually Republicans.

Taking a cut-off point for COPE ratings is always a little arbitrary. There is no magic number which guarantees congressmen endorsement, though a rare 100 per cent correct figure helps. One useful dividing line, however, is the figure of 90 per cent correct. In practice, 90 per cent provides us with a satisfactory sample of the fifth of congressmen most in line with COPE. Their characteristics are striking, and not always predictable. First, congressmen scoring over 90 are almost always Democrats. In 1966, 92 congressmen scored over 90 per cent on COPE's scale; all were Democrats. In 1972, 101 congressmen scored over 90 per cent correct; all but two were Democrats. Second, congressmen who win the approval of COPE tend to be popular with groups associated with the liberal wing of the Democratic party. In 1966, for example, the Democrats scoring over 90 with COPE averaged 83 per cent with the liberal cause group, Americans for Democratic Action. Though, for reasons which will be discussed later, the correlation between ADA and COPE ratings of congressmen and senators has fallen from 0.98 in 1960 to 0.84 in 1974, the fit between them is still very close. The average ADA score for congressmen in 1966 was only 44 per cent. Third, and rather surprisingly, COPE's favourite legislators do not necessarily have a large number of blue collar workers in their districts. In 1972, 54 out of the 101 congressmen scoring over 90 per cent with COPE had *fewer* than the national mean number of blue collar workers in their districts. COPE's scale tends to pick out unusually liberal Democratic congressmen who may or may not represent districts which contain many blue collar workers.[16]

Is this coincidence? Does COPE happen to rate liberal Democrats highly or is this deliberate? Meany has always argued that the high proportion of congressmen rated highly, and therefore endorsed by COPE, who are Democrats is accidental. In 1955, Meany told reporters that he would not tie the AFL-CIO to either party. In practice, they would support more Democrats than Republicans 'because that probably will be just the way it works out'.[17] Republicans remain sceptical. Catchpole, a conservative critic, noted that COPE's founding director, McDevitt, though coming from the Pennsylvania AFL and not the CIO, was not only consistently liberal, but also a partisan Democrat and anti-Republican. McDevitt had described the contrast between Roosevelt and the moderate Republican, Willkie, as that between 'the New Deal philosophy personified by Roosevelt and arrogance, selfishness and greed as personified by Willkie'.[18] An article in a business magazine on COPE in 1963 also charged that COPE was a surrogate for the Democratic Party. Margaret Chase Smith, Republican Senator from Maine, complained that even though she had scored over 80 per cent with COPE, it still endorsed her opponent.[19] Representative Glenn Cunningham, also a Republican, complained that his local COPE had been willing to back him, but had been dissuaded by national officials. Not until 1974 did COPE endorse a Republican in a Senate race and the first such candidate, Richard Schweiker of Pennsylvania, had, after all, a 100 per cent correct COPE record.

The truth or falseness of the accusations that COPE is really an off-shoot of the Democratic Party could lead us well off the subject of COPE and on to that of the next chapter, namely the role of labour in the Democratic Party. The main relevance of the charges here is that their widespread currency strengthens our picture of COPE as a force working predominantly to strengthen liberal Democrats.

THE IMPACT OF COPE

What difference does COPE make to the outcome of elections? One of the commonplaces of American voting behaviour is that members of unions and their families are more likely to vote Democratic than blue collar workers who are not. Thus in the 1976 election, Ford marginally out-polled Carter amongst blue collar workers. But Carter won two-thirds of the votes of union members and their families.[20] Of course, though COPE backed Carter energetically, we cannot conclude that it was COPE which made the difference. There are, for a start, the political campaigns run by individual unions, a topic to which we shall turn shortly. Then there are problems in determining the direction of causality. Is it that union members are unusually likely to be Democrats, or that Democrats are unusually likely to be union members? Or, alternatively, do certain other factors (such as region, or the nature of the plant in which the voter works) cause certain people to be both union members and Democrats?

Such questions are hard to answer both in practice and in principle. There is also comparatively little evidence to guide us. However, certain propositions can be advanced with a limited amount of supporting evidence. First, COPE does make a difference to turnout and re-gistration. Workers are unlikely to register, let alone vote, in the same proportions as the electorate as a whole. As we have seen in Connecticut, a good COPE campaign can reverse this trend.[21] Second, there is some evidence that some workers do take note of what organised labour has to say. Unfortunately, most of the surveys concentrate not on the impact of COPE but of the UAW in its strongest areas. Nonetheless, the findings of such studies provide some guidance.

The first and pioneering research in this field was conducted by Kornhauser, Sheppard and Mayer.[22] Selecting Detroit, where the influence of the UAW could be expected to be unusually strong, the authors tended to undermine the political importance of the union. Only 7 per cent of their respondents listed the UAW as the most important source of information on candidates (p. 88) and only 23 per cent of the union's members understood its stand on a complex re-appointment referendum (p. 71). On the other hand, registration was unusually high in union areas (p. 31), the membership trusted and supported the political work of their leaders (p. 262), the tendency for blue collar workers not to vote was overcome (p. 264), and at least 35 per cent of the information received about Democratic candidates had come via the UAW or CIO.

Sheppard and Masters[23] updated the study in 1959. They found that the UAW had succeeded in registering 90 per cent of its members, and 87 per cent actually voted. Rather surprisingly, 67 per cent of their sample chose 'unions' from a list including business groups, churches and fraternal organisations as organisations where 'you'd be more likely to vote for candidates they recommend'. A further study in another town where the UAW is strong (Toledo, Ohio) found that 16 per cent of respondents cited the union and 11 per cent the union journal as the source of their political ideas.[24] As the present author would expect the answer to be 'zero' to both questions, these figures seem quite impressive. It is often thought, too, that the unions can be successful in returning their members to normal party allegiance. The major effort the unions made to persuade their members to vote for Humphrey, not Wallace, in 1968 was after all one of the major reasons why Humphrey almost defeated Nixon.[25] By November, most union members were back in the Democratic fold.

It is important to emphasise that the surveys quoted were conducted with the UAW, not COPE, in mind. Moreover, the most important, Kornhauser's, was completed before COPE existed. Nonetheless, they suggest a picture of the labour union as having a minor but significant influence over its members' votes.

However, the close links between the COPE and Congressional Democrats links COPE to the fortunes of that Party. Good years for the Democrats are likely to be good years for COPE. The success rate claimed by the AFL-CIO is shown in Table 2.4. Though COPE successes were steady in the House (where incumbency provides a strong advantage), its success rate dipped sharply in 1966 and in 1968 in elections for governors and senators (which are more competitive). The years 1966 and 1968 were particularly bad ones for Democrats; the dip in COPE's success rate indicates that it cannot reverse broad trends benefiting or handicapping the Democrats.

One useful test of the power of COPE would be its ability to transfer votes between parties. Unfortunately, because COPE rarely endorses Republicans, such cases are rare. An interesting case occurred in 1972,

TABLE 2.4: *Percentage Success Rate in Nominations for (number of successful nominees in brackets)*

Year	Governor	Senate	House
1960	60.9 (23)	66.7 (24)	53.7 (296)
1962	58.3 (24)	69.0 (29)	57.8 (334)
1964	63.6 (22)	80.6 (31)	66.9 (237)
1966	28.6 (28)	40.9 (22)	54.0 (337)
1968	35.3 (17)	55.6 (17)	57.6 (323)
1970	65.5 (29)	61.3 (31)	60.4 (336)
1972	64.7 (17)	55.2 (29)	59.9 (362)
1974	78.8 (33)	75.8 (33)	69.2 (389)

Source: AFL-CIO *Federationist*, September 1975 Vol. 82, No. 9.

however, when COPE endorsed a Republican for the first time in a state-wide contest when it supported Richard Schweiker's bid to win re-election to the Senate. Schweiker had an almost perfect voting record as far as COPE was concerned. Nonetheless, he was a Republican. Would workers vote for him? The evidence is that they did. Whereas 72.9 per cent of union voters supported the Democratic candidate for Governor whom COPE endorsed, Milton Shapp, 73.9 per cent supported the Republican, Schweiker, for the Senate. An impressive transfer of votes had been achieved even though 61.8 per cent of union voters identified with the Democratic Party. Those voting for the union 'ticket' of Shapp and Schweiker included 58.3 per cent of those with a high party identification.[26] Though the AFL-CIO (and Schweiker) were pleased by the result, it does not indicate the power of COPE alone. Schweiker was an incumbent. His voting record as one of the Senate's most liberal Republicans pleased his constituents as well as unions. Schweiker's own campaign had helped to separate him from his party. (Schweiker was subsequently to deny in an interview that the AFL-CIO should endorse many other Republicans because 'they're all too damn conservative'.) Thus Schweiker may have received many union votes by his efforts alone. Yet it is hard to deny COPE some credit for the unusually high proportion of the union vote Schweiker won. Schweiker took 53.3 per cent of the vote overall, but 73.9 per cent of the votes of union members. COPE must have helped create that contrast.

COPE: TRENDS AND PROSPECTS

Ten years ago, the prospects for COPE seemed bright or, from a conservative viewpoint, daunting. The organisation's efficiency seemed likely to carry on improving while its officials had a clear sense of destiny, to be 'the mass party of liberalism',[27] as one union leader put it. Events since then, particularly the breaks with liberals over Vietnam and with the Democratic Party when it nominated George McGovern, have weakened COPE's sense of purpose. They have also weakened COPE's institutional position.

RIVAL ORGANISATIONS

The most obvious way in which COPE has been weakened has been the increased tendency for individual unions to develop an independent political capability. Individual unions never abandoned their own efforts to influence the voting behaviour of their members. Yet as COPE blossomed and improved its technique, so individual unions had less incentive to spend money on elections, except where a sectional interest was involved (as with the Maritime Unions and the Congressional Merchant Marine and Fisheries Committees). The United Auto Workers retained the tradition of political action and the machinery to pursue it. Moreover, the constant friction between its President, Reuther, and Meany suggested that it would be unwise to leave COPE as the only political vehicle for organised labour. Yet the Reuther brothers tended to see the alternative to COPE not in the UAW but in the Industrial Union Department of the AFL-CIO, the unit Reuther had intended to be the continuance of the CIO within labour's united front.

The revival of independent electoral action by individual unions dates back to the departure of the UAW from the AFL-CIO. The breach, handled in a way which maximised ill-feeling, was due to personal friction between Reuther and Meany and policy differences which began with Reuther's unhappiness with the uncritical support by the AFL-CIO for American involvement in Vietnam, but which Reuther rapidly broadened into an argument about the political role of the AFL-CIO at home and abroad.[28]

Reuther suffered a defeat when the UAW withdrew from the AFL-CIO; a defeat which was obscured by his early death in an air crash. No former CIO Unions followed the UAW's example. In spite of an unworthy and counter-productive alliance with the Teamsters, Reuther failed to establish any alternative structure to the AFL-CIO. His successor, Leonard Woodcock, was less flamboyant and independent as a leader; both the UAW's Washington lobbyists and its local electoral action officials quietly resumed working with the AFL-CIO. In 1972, however, the trend towards independent union action was strengthened. Partly by force of personality, Meany secured a massive vote of those present at the AFL-CIO Executive Council against endorsing McGovern. Only Jerry Wurf (of the AFSCME), Al Grosspiron of the Oil, Chemical and Atomic Workers, and Paul Jennings of the International Union of Electricians actually voted against Meany, whereas 27 voted with him.[29]

The meagre three votes for McGovern obscured the hostility to Meany's policy. Some, perhaps overwhelmed by Meany, stated that though they would vote against the AFL-CIO endorsing McGovern, their individual unions would not. Thus Floyd Smith of the International Association of Machinists (IAM) and Alex Rohan of the Printing Press union both voted against the AFL-CIO endorsing McGovern, and yet campaigned actively with their unions for him. Others, too, felt bitter and frustrated by COPE's failure to oppose Nixon. Joe Beirne of the Communications Workers had violent disagreements with the chief of COPE, Al Barkan, accusing him of being 'asleep' during the 1972 nominating process.[30] A commentator noted that 'a whole generation of political leaders is discovering political independence and enjoying it'.[31]

Those most annoyed by Meany's line in 1972 decided that never again would labour unions effectively be blocked by the AFL-CIO from supporting a Democrat. The disaffected took a number of steps. First, individual unions started to develop an independent political machine. Thus AFSCME trained 900 people for electoral action independent of COPE.[32] Second, the disaffected unions cut back on their subscriptions to COPE and the personnel they seconded to it during campaigns. Third, they formed an alliance, the Labour Coalition Clearinghouse,[33] to coordinate their efforts in the 1976 primaries and elections. Unions affiliated were the UAW; Communications Workers of America; Electrical Workers; Oil, Chemical and Atomic Workers; Graphic Arts; United Mineworkers; and the National Education Association.

The Labor Coalition was never as well equipped as COPE. Nor was it able to agree on one candidate for the Democratic nomination for President. Yet its existence has had a sharp effect, dealing COPE a double blow. First, the unions within the Labor Coalition, also members of the AFL-CIO, had been the most reliable subscribers to COPE. Many, perhaps a majority, of the unions within the AFL-CIO fail to meet the subscription target for funds for political action set for them. Unions such as AFSCME and IAM in contrast regularly meet, and sometimes exceed, that target. Second, the unions which subscribe regularly to COPE also provide the troops on the ground to man the telephone banks, register voters and persuade them to vote. When the unions within the AFL-CIO affiliated to the Labor Coalition, they took with them many of COPE's most loyal workers. The poor showing that COPE made in the Pennsylvania primary was attributed by COPE's officers to the fact that the Labor Coalition had robbed it of its best helpers. The Labor Coalition also took significant resources, such as money and manpower, which would otherwise have gone to COPE.

Whether the Labor Coalition will continue to exist is uncertain. The coalition undoubtedly lost some of its *raison d'être* in 1976 when the AFL-CIO once more backed the Democratic nominee for President, though he was not its first choice. More to the point is whether COPE continues to avoid participation in Democratic Party primaries. So long as it does, the Labor Coalition will provide a valuable instrument for unions who object to this boycott. Whether or not individual unions will revert to placing their faith in COPE is a different matter. Only the departure of Meany and the COPE director, Al Barkan, and their replacement by people more sympathetic to the liberal wing of the Democratic Party would convince the most political of the Unions within the AFL-CIO that they could afford to place reliance on COPE. The Labor Coalition itself can be easily over-estimated; the trend towards independent political action by unions should not be neglected.

This trend has been reinforced by the campaign finance reform legislation enacted after Watergate. In spite of the difficulties with the Federal Election Commission described at the start of the chapter, campaign finance reforms benefit unions. By limiting funds spent on advertising, campaign finance reforms reinforce the importance of organisation. To the extent that candidates cannot rely on expensive television advertisements to reach voters, they are forced back on more traditional techniques such as canvassing in which COPE specialises. Nor are the federal grants to candidates sufficient to avoid this stringency. The Carter presidential campaign was run in some states on a budget less than that hitherto thought to be necessary for a House campaign.[34] Labour, of course, above all provides organisation to help its friends. The efforts of COPE to mobilise support for a candidate do not count towards his campaign budget; nor do the efforts of such AFL-CIO off-shoots as the A. Philip Randolph which concentrates on mobilising black voters. COPE or union organisational aid to a candidate is both a free and a costless benefit whose value has been increased by campaign finance reform.

One provision of campaign finance law, as interpreted by the Supreme Court, has affected already the balance between COPE and constituent unions, however. That provision stipulates that no one may give a candidate or his campaign organisation more than $5,000. The effect of this is that there is no longer any point in unions concentrating campaign contributions in the hands of COPE, for COPE can give only $5,000 to any one campaign. In contrast, each individual union can give $5,000 to a campaign. The optimal strategy, therefore, is for individual unions to limit their contribution to COPE, and to make individual contributions to candidates they favour. Ten unions acting independently can give $50,000 to a candidate; COPE is limited to $5,000. Thus legislation currently in force will strengthen the tendency – unleashed by Meany's refusal to endorse George McGovern – for political action by labour to be based more on individual unions than COPE.

Yet the future for political action by organised labour is bright. When labour activists discussed forming a labour party in the United States, an insuperable problem seemed to be the strength of party loyalty amongst voters. The traditionally Democratic (or Republican) voter would not be shifted easily from his or her allegiance. Moreover, the grip of 'machines' on many cities in the United States was strong. The creation of a 'labour' party is not on the agenda anymore. Yet the barriers to effective political action have almost disappeared, too. Voters are increasingly willing to 'split their tickets' between the two parties. The proportion of Americans identifying with the two major parties has declined drastically. The 'machine' is almost a thing of the past. Individual voters are increasingly aware of, and motivated by, issues not party labels.[35] In this context, labour unions can come into their own. Their ability to promote candidates among not only the electorate but the population at large has probably never been greater. The willingness of the electorate to respond to appeals based on issues has also never been greater. Provided they remain reasonably united, labour unions can exert more influence on elections than ever before.

3 Labour and the Democratic Party

A profound ambiguity has always characterised the relationship between the labour unions and the Democratic Party. George Meany has embodied this ambiguity throughout his Presidency of the AFL-CIO. On the one hand, Meany has repeated closely Gompers' attitude to politics. Labour, Meany wrote in 1966, should follow Gompers' dictum of rewarding friends and punishing enemies. 'I don't buy the idea, and there is nothing to sustain it, that labor needs the Democratic Party. I'm sure it is the other way around,'[1] Meany added. As far back as the time of the creation of the AFL-CIO, Meany stated that, 'We absolutely refuse to allow ourselves to be an appendage of the Democratic Party.'[2] Indeed, Meany's biographer tells us that Meany was so irked by the assumption by Democrats that labour was tied to them, the power of the Southern Democrats and their 'rudeness' to him that Meany opposed – unsuccessfully – endorsing Stevenson in 1956.[3] On the other hand, the hard fact is that Democrats are much more likely than Republicans to support labour's objectives. Meany recognised this dilemma in an interview with the Washington D.C., *Evening Star* in 1955. Meany said that he refused to tie the AFL to either party, but he felt constrained to add that it would back more Democrats than Republicans 'because that probably will be just the way it works out'.[4] During the Kennedy and Johnson years, Meany was very close to the Democratic Presidents. The warmth of Meany's attachment to Kennedy was matched by the frequency of his conferences with Johnson. Indeed, Meany's biographer describes how, at a reception for the most important Democrats at the Chicago convention, Meany stood receiving guests for an hour *'enjoying his recognised eminence in the Democratic Party'*[5] (emphasis added).

Is the AFL-CIO part of the Democratic Party or not? It is worth remembering that not only labour unions but the Party itself have changed over the years. Many of the quotations which can be presented to show how suspicious unions were of the Democratic Party before

1960 do not provide evidence of union conservatism. The reliance of the old American parties on ethnic, religious and regional divisions could not but pose problems for a labour union. The Gompers strategy of avoiding associations with either party was but a sensible avoidance of emotions which would divide the members of unions. Indeed, as late as the 1950s and Stevenson's attempts for the Presidency, it remained uncertain whether the Democratic party would progress towards being more a party of liberalism or would continue efforts to conciliate the Southern wing. Stevenson himself seemed to favour the latter strategy to a surprising degree.[6] The Southern Democrats dominated Congress by holding the most important positions such as Majority Leader in the Senate, Speaker of the House and committee chairman-ships in both chambers as well as seats on the most strategic committees themselves, such as the House Rules. Moreover, the liberal wing of the Republican Party was not as small and isolated in the 1950s as it was to become. Rockefeller was but the most plausible of those 'liberals' hoping for the Republican nomination; Republican Senators such as Keating (New York) were loyal members of a civil rights coalition which was opposed by shamelessly racist Democrats. Even outside the South, Democrats have not always been liberal. When George Meany worked to put the support of the AFL behind LaGuardia in New York in 1933, and not behind the Democratic Party, he was unquestionably working to back the more liberal candidate.[7]

From the end of the Second World War to the late 1960s, the links between labour and the Democratic Party grew ever closer. The passage of Taft-Hartley not only gave labour unions good reason to dislike the Republicans, but, as we have seen, it also mobilised the unions politically. That political mobilisation, channelled into COPE, benefited Democrats overwhelmingly. In 1956, 1960, 1964 and 1968, Democratic Presidential candidates received significant support from the AFL-CIO. No Republican received COPE help in a Senate contest until COPE helped Richard Schweiker in Pennsylvania in 1974, and only a handful of Republicans have ever received help in House elections. On the other hand, even the most liberal and politically-minded unions abandoned in the 1940s any real interest in the idea of a Labour Party. One of the most obvious reasons for this loss of interest was the belief that the ties of party identification felt by voters precluded the creation of a new party. As time passed, though, party identification weakened, but the need for a separate party also diminished. The 1958 mid-term elections brought in a particularly large influx of non-Southern, liberal Democrats. The trend has continued so that by today even seniority—the practice of appointing the person from the majority party who has sat on a committee continuously the longest as chairman—which so long favoured the South, has begun to favour more liberal regions. In the House of Representatives in 1946 the Democratic Party was two-thirds composed of Southern Democrats; in 1976, two-thirds of House Democrats were from outside the South. Even the Southerners have become less dogmatically conservative, probably under the impact of the 1965 Voting Rights Act and the sharp rise in the proportion of blacks in the South who register and vote. Democratic Presidential nominees since Roosevelt have clearly and consistently been more liberal than their Republican rivals, being prepared if necessary (with the possible exception of Stevenson) to lose ground in the South. All these trends brought more of the Democratic Party into line with the policies of the AFL-CIO.

The relationship between the bulk of the Democratic Party and the AFL-CIO has long been close. The leaders of the AFL-CIO either attended, or were in close touch with Democratic conventions. Meany expected to be consulted about who the Democratic nominee should be. His wishes were not always respected. Thus, ironically in view of their later friendship, Meany was very upset by the selection of Johnson as Kennedy's running mate, but Johnson was nonetheless selected.[8] Yet, and not by accident, no Democratic nominee between 1956 and 1972 was unacceptable to the leadership of the AFL-CIO. At the start of the period, in 1956, the Executive Council voted by only fourteen votes to eight to endorse Stevenson with the eight dissenters doubting whether Stevenson was sufficiently different from the almost certain victor, Eisenhower, to make involvement worthwhile. At the end of the period, McGovern was rejected (with only three out of thirty-five possible votes in his favour) because he was too radical. In between, the party professionals, who dominated the party conventions, were well aware of the need to nominate a candidate capable of winning both the labour vote and the organisational backing of the AFL-CIO. Meany and the AFL-CIO Executive wallowed in the luxury of having what they believed to be a *de facto* veto over the Democratic nomination without being nominally part of the party. Whether Meany in fact did enjoy a veto over the Democratic Party's nominee is an interesting question. The failure of Kefauver in 1956 certainly demonstrates that an outsider' could not force himself on the party as became possible after 1968; even Kennedy's success was based to a significant degree on courting party regulars. It is very definitely the case that since the AFL-CIO merger in 1955, the party establishment would not have wished to saddle themselves with a candidate unwelcome to Meany, though neither would liberals have thought it natural to support someone unwelcome to Meany until late in the 1960s.

Relations at the local level by and large paralleled this pattern of nominal separation but practical cooperation. J. David Greenstone charted a pattern showing that the balance of power between the Democratic Party and labour unions varied from city to city.[9] In Chicago, the machine was dominant; in Detroit labour practically *was* the Democratic Party. Everywhere, the unions looked to, and worked with, the Democrats to the disadvantage of Republicans. In some places the unions could pick the candidate; in others they had to take the one who was going. Nowhere did unions look naturally to Republicans though here and there Republicans such as Rockefeller as Governor of New York could entice away individual unions (such as the construction unions) by careful and massive manipulation with state government contracts.

Such was the situation prior to the tensions of the late 1960s. Broadly speaking what happened then was that a group emerged within the Democratic Party which was not totally new in its ideology but was new in its strength. This group I shall term 'the new liberals'. Throughout the 1950s, the civil rights movement had been gaining in strength. During the early 1960s, civil rights campaigners adopted increasingly militant tactics including mass marches (e.g. on Washington in 1963) and the original 'sit-ins' at segregated lunch counters in the South. Both the marches and the 'sit-ins' attracted not only blacks but some white middle-class professionals and, numerically more important, students. When the 1965 Voting Rights Act, with its assumption of responsibility for registering blacks as well as desegregating facilities by the Justice Department, was passed, civil rights activism became less necessary. At that very moment, however, opposition to the 'escalation' of American involvement in Vietnam began to gain strength on the campuses. A new force had emerged, 'the young'. Education, spare time and money made 'the young' (who were really college students) a potent force behind the new liberals. By 1968, the students had learnt the political game so well that in the snows of New Hampshire they provided crucial help when Senator Eugene McCarthy humiliated President Johnson, whose poor showing helped force him into retirement.

Few in the labour unions viewed the emergence of 'the young' as a political force with equanimity. Even that most liberal and political of unions, the UAW, was less certain than the new liberals in its opposition to American involvement in the war. The top leadership of the AFL-

CIO was non-flagging in its support for President Johnson and his policies. Meany was, after all, one of Johnson's confidants. Even the UAW's tenuous suggestions that the United States should show more interest in a negotiated settlement were greeted with violent denunciations from Meany; the peace movement was beyond the pale.

Not only were there differences on specific policies between the new liberals and labour; there was also an enormous cultural gap between the labour leaders and the anti-war movement. The labour movement fought for a place for their members in the American dream; the students seemed to reject the dream most blue collar workers had yet to experience. The labour leaders were accustomed to stressing their patriotism and respect for law; the students burnt the American flag and accepted illegal action as a legitimate tactic. Meany, of course, expressed vehemently many of the disdainful attitudes to 'the young' which many labour leaders felt. In 1970 Meany, talking about differences between the generations, commented that young people 'smoke more pot than we do' and are inclined to 'lay around a field in Woodstock New York' (a reference to the famous festival). Meany concluded, 'I am not going to trust the destiny of the country to that group.'[10]

Equally, if not more reprehensible, was the prejudice which the educated, predominantly middle class students felt against labour. It became a firmly believed 'fact' that blue collar workers were racial bigots, 'hawks' in foreign policy and hostile to civil liberties. Research was to establish that the blue collar worker was no more bigoted, hawkish or intolerant than the average American.[11] Yet such research came too late to avoid the prejudice contributing to a politically significant breach between labour and the new sort of liberals in the anti-war movement. To the anti-war movement, the blue collar workers were, as Ben Wattenberg commented, 'beery, hawkish, ethnic slobs'.[12] Not surprisingly, blue collar workers tended not to respond kindly to such a caricature.

If the division between liberals and labour had existed only on Vietnam, a reconciliation or *modus vivendi* could have been achieved. The 'doveish' views of many of the AFL-CIO's favourite congressmen such as James O'Hara or Frank Thompson did not preclude good relations continuing between them and organised labour. Unfortunately, the concerns which the new liberals felt about other than the Vietnam War were not close to labour's heart. In theory labour had long been interested in laws to protect the consumer or prevent pollution. Yet in practice labour leaders did not attach the highest priority to them, preferring to concentrate on social issues such as anti-poverty legislation or national health insurance. In contrast, the new liberals were very interested in tightening up consumer protection (making Ralph Nader their saint), cleaner government (creating a new group, Common Cause, to work for it) and showed much less interest in social issues. When the new liberals did turn to social issues, their interests were in helping the very poorest classes, such as the ghetto dweller or migrant farm worker, assuming that the blue collar workers' problems had been solved already, overlooking the fact that most blue collar workers in America do not enjoy a wonderful or particularly affluent life style.[13] So, the new liberals tended to propose policies to help the very poorest (such as bussing or a quota system for employment) whose costs were borne by the blue collar worker. By the early 1970s, skilled commentators, such as Scammon and Wattenberg,[14] could claim plausibly that there was a new policy divide based on 'the social issue'. This category included a number of issues such as law enforcement, bussing and questions of personal behaviour on which blue collar workers felt that the 'new liberals' were not their friends but their opponents. New liberal theorists, such as Fred Dutton, reciprocated, arguing that in the struggle for a liberated society, the college-educated would be opposed by the working class.

The Democratic Party became the battleground for the new liberals and labour. Labour was *de facto* in the Democratic Party; the anti-war activists understandably felt that as liberals their home was in that party too. As is well known, the anti-war movement initially suffered major reverses in their attempts to accumulate delegates. Both Eugene McCarthy and Robert Kennedy found that their successes in primaries were not matched by success in accumulating delegates at the convention. The party regulars were well capable of suffering a reverse in a primary only to capture, as in New York[15] a high proportion of that state's delegates. Hubert Humphrey, heir-apparent to President Johnson and, as an old style liberal, the darling of organised labour, was the beneficiary. As a further contribution to the bitterness that was to divide the party, the young idealistic protesters against the war who followed Eugene McCarthy to his defeat at the Chicago convention of 1968, were clubbed and gassed by Mayor Daley's police in what an official report by the Kerner Commission was subsequently to term a police riot.

Yet the new liberals were to arise phoenix-like from Chicago. One of the least-noticed decisions at that traumatic convention was to establish a commission on delegate selection chaired by Senator McGovern

(South Dakota), the final bearer of the assassinated Robert Kennedy's banner. The response of organised labour to the McGovern Commission is, with hindsight, extraordinary. Putting up almost no fight at all, the AFL-CIO seemed to sulk in its corner waiting for the party to come, as Meany saw it, to its senses. As early as August 1970, Meany pronounced the Democratic Party 'a shambles' which was 'disintegrating '. The New Left, Meany said, was taking over and this would offend his members 'who believe in the American system and maybe have a greater stake in it than 15, 20 years ago'.[16] Far from resisting such an awful threat, Meany let it happen. The archives of the McGovern–Fraser Commission (Congressman Donald Fraser replaced McGovern as chairman) contain no substantial criticism of the Commission's proposals by organised labour.[17] More importantly, I. W. Abel, President of the Steelworkers Union, close confidant of Meany and nominally a member of the Commission, boycotted its sessions. (Some argue this was due to his pique at not being allowed to send a staff member to represent him.) His failure to attend was sometimes crucial. For example, Meany was subsequently to criticise the adoption by the Commission of quotas to increase the representation of blacks, the young and women. Yet quotas had been adopted by only one vote; Abel could have stopped them had he attended.[18]

Why did the AFL-CIO set itself against the Commission and all its works so vehemently? In the first place, the AFL-CIO leaders, like many others, believed either that the Commission would come up with little, or that its proposals would be buried quietly. More important, however, was the speed with which it became apparent that the Commission was concerned with increasing the representation of groups which did not include labour, possibly by quotas which are an anathema to unions in the workplace where they undermine solidarity, and that it intended to recommend a more participatory system of delegate selection.

A participatory system of delegate selection has caused two problems for Meany and his adherents. First, he has objected to open COPE involvement in Democratic primaries because it would mark a step away from the Gompers tradition of bipartisanship. To participate in primaries is to step firmly and finally into the Democratic Party, a step Meany has always resisted. Second, Meany and the chief of COPE, Barkan, believe that workers are disadvantaged in a participatory system. Workers are less willing and able than middle class groups, such as university lecturers, to attend caucus meetings to select delegates which last into the early hours of the morning; they are also less likely to participate in primaries. In short, Meany and Barkan believe that a participatory system reduces the power of labour and increases that of the middle class radical. Now not all unions believe this. Local labour leaders in Michigan and Ohio in fact argued in testimony to the McGovern Commission that the closed system which existed until 1972 reduced the influence of organised labour;[19] AFSCME, the UAW, IAM (International Association of Machinists) and other liberal, politically active unions agree. Their leaders argue that primaries are ideally suited to labour's political machine, and that if participation in primaries is a formal admission that organised labour is part of the Democratic Party, then that is no more than honest admission of the truth.

George Meany, however, did not agree. Indeed, from 1969–74, Meany explored unsuccessfully the possibility of links with the Republican Party. In 1969, Meany and other AFL-CIO leaders began 'intimate' discussions with the new Republican administration at White Sulphur Springs, West Virginia,[20] on the national economic situation. In 1970, Meany praised Nixon's attitude on some labour issues and said that relations were good, 'but no love feast'.[21] In fairness to Meany, we should remember that he added that Nixon's attitudes on general public policy issues, especially civil rights, were unsatisfactory. Finally, in February 1973, Nixon paid a formal but very cordial visit to the AFL-CIO Executive Council.[22] Yet the explorations were never successful. Nixon's policies could be embraced only both at the cost of breaking faith with the labour movement's political traditions and, though Meany was slower to realise this, at a cost to labour's own interests. Nixon's general economic policies were not advantageous to labour; some of his individual decisions, such as his nomination of Haynsworth for the Supreme Court when Haynsworth was not only racist but also anti-union showed how limited were the chances of an AFL-CIO/Republican alliance. Unfortunately, this was not apparent until after the 1972 elections.

The 1972 elections brought the breach between the new liberals and the AFL-CIO to a traumatic climax. The AFL-CIO Executive voted overwhelmingly (27 to 3 with 5 absent) to remain neutral in the election, denying its support to the Democratic nominee, George McGovern. Why did the AFL-CIO do it? A number of reasons can be advanced. Certainly the membership was unenthusiastic about McGovern; yet defections to Wallace in 1968 had served merely to increase the AFL-CIO's efforts on behalf of the Democratic nomineee, Humphrey.[23] It was said that McGovern had let labour down in 1965 when he broke his word and opposed a move to end a filibuster on repeal of Section 14(b) of Taft-Hartley. Yet over the years McGovern had achieved high COPE ratings and had proved a good friend to organised labour. As such, COPE had no doubts about backing McGovern in 1974 in his efforts to be re-elected to the Senate from South Dakota.[24]

It was also said that the AFL-CIO could not support McGovern as there was no unanimity in the Executive Council. This was not merely an inadequate reason (there had been no unanimity about supporting Stevenson in 1956)[25] but highly misleading. Meany worked hard to secure a unanimous rejection of McGovern. Thus he prevailed on Floyd Smith of the International Association of Machinists (IAM) and Alex Rohan of the Printing Press Men to vote against McGovern in the Executive Council, though they subsequently committed their unions to his cause.[26] Only three union leaders voted to endorse McGovern – Wurf of the American Federation of State, County and Municipal Employees (AFSCME); Paul Jennings of the Union of Electricians (UE); and Al Grosspiron of the Oil, Chemical and Atomic Workers. Wurf himself attributed the vote at the Council above all to the personal loyalty of the Council's members to Meany.

It is puzzling, therefore, why Meany opposed McGovern so implacably, a McGovern with a 100 per cent COPE record in 1972 against a Nixon not only with a 13 per cent COPE record and but also a President whom the AFL-CIO would wish to see impeached within two years. Indeed, in February 1971, Meany had said he would accept any of the Democratic candidates, including McGovern, except Wallace, who was 'racist right down to the soles of his feet'.[27] Wurf was undoubtedly correct in attributing Meany's hostility 'more to how McGovern won the nomination than with his record before or during the campaign'.[28] Meany disliked McGovern's strategy of winning the nomination through the use of anti-war activists, the 'new liberals', to exploit the opportunities the more participatory system (especially in caucus states) his Commission had helped shape. Seeing that by August McGovern seemed bound to lose, Meany saw no reason to help him. Indeed, a crushing defeat of McGovern might bring the party back to its senses, and restore a system in which labour enjoyed power within the party, thus wielding an invisible but effective veto without bearing the responsibility. Any emotional loyalty to the Democratic Party was swept away by such thinking as that of the *New York Times* editorialist who celebrated McGovern's victory as a defeat for 'Big Cities, Big Labor and Big South with its heavy and often baleful influence'.[29] Meany felt, with much justice, that his political record over the years was very different from 'Big South's'. Liberals who did not see this (or whose followers could not) did not deserve his support.

How badly the refusal of the AFL-CIO to endorse McGovern hurt him is almost impossible to calculate. Certainly, the fact that he was deprived of COPE's support deprived McGovern of the help of a skilled organisation, when his own was weak. Beyond this, however, was the more ambiguous part that the AFL-CIO's position played in reinforcing the hostility or suspicion which already existed towards McGovern amongst the white working class. McGovern suffered the worst defeat of any Presidential candidate this century. The magnitude of the defeat opened the possibility that the Democratic Party would cast off the reforms and policies which appalled Meany and which he always hoped would be discredited in defeat.

To a limited extent, the Democratic Party did renounce McGovernism. McGovern's choice as party chairman, Jean Westwood, was rapidly replaced by Robert Strauss, a more conservative Texan, skilled in reconciliation. More important to the future of the party than this symbolic change was whether the Democratic Party would please Meany and Barkan by a renunciation of the new delegate selection system and, in particular, quotas. The issue was to be settled at the first Democratic mid-term convention in Kansas City in 1974. Unlike the situation in 1972, the AFL-CIO neither spurned the delegate selection system, nor overlooked its importance. As a result, labour was well represented, though in some states (e.g. Pennsylvania), prominent labour leaders were not chosen as delegates. During 1973, AFL-CIO people had been moving quietly back into participation in the party's politics, and were hoping for success in turning the party back to its old ways.

The task which confronted the leadership of the AFL-CIO in December 1974 at Kansas City was difficult. Unlike Meany and Barkan, most of the delegates to the convention were stunned, not gratified by the magnitude of the party's defeat; they were also aware that the Republicans had unexpectedly become very vulnerable if only Democratic unity could maintained. Nixon, who had vanquished McGovern in 1972, had just resigned the Presidency in ignominy; the Republican Party, which had not itself benefited from Nixon's landslide, was now afflicted by a backlash over Watergate and the state of the economy. The convention met, therefore, in a mood of reconciliation.[30] Mayor Daley, who had previously figured large in the demonology of the new liberals, was politely, even warmly received, particularly as he made clear his acceptance of the new order. The *New York Times* felt that 'a fragile spirit of conciliation' prevailed as Strauss had succeeded in quietening passions.[31] In this climate, reversing the method of delegate selection was not on. The rapid increase in the number of states using the primary system presented Meany with a *fait accompli* he was powerless to reverse. In any case, arguments that participation was undesirable were hard to sustain in the 1970s. The most that Meany and Barkan could achieve, therefore, was the abolition of quotas.

It may not be obvious why unions felt so strongly about quotas. As we shall see elsewhere, even at the very moment when the AFL-CIO was in the throes of the drive for civil rights legislation in 1963, it had still opposed quotas. Quotas have aroused instinctive opposition in the American labour movement because of their undesirability from the viewpoint of union strategy in industrial relations. By their very nature, quotas emphasise racial or ethnic rather than class loyalty. Even worse, their application is likely to weaken hallowed union principles such as seniority (first in, last out) which unions see as an invaluable barrier to employer tyranny. Beyond this, however, quotas aroused hostility in the AFL-CIO for two more general reasons. First, quotas seemed to suggest that the cost of ameliorating the condition of blacks would be borne by the white working class. White workers would be discriminated against to achieve black advance; white middle class liberals might applaud this, but were themselves well insulated by qualifications from this process. Yet white workers were arguably only a rung or two above most blacks on the ladder. Why should they be the ones to pay the price of social justice? Second, quotas for blacks, women and the young were not accompanied by quotas for labour. Yet workers are hardly over-represented at party conventions, in spite of the crucial importance of their support for the Democratic Party. If the 1972 election result had proved anything, it was the folly of the argument that in the 'new politics', so-called minorities such as women, blacks and the young could provide a better electoral base than the New Deal Coalition. Thus a labour spokesman at Kansas City noted bitterly that 'not a line' in the proposed Party Charter mentions labour 'without whose united and massive campaign action this Party will not win in 1976 or any other election year'.[32]

At first, the Convention seemed likely to gratify Meany and Barkan. In place of setting quotas of 'minorities' for delegations to party conventions to achieve, the relevant part of the Party Charter, X(6), merely called for affirmative action. Indeed, the section specifically stated that 'composition [of a delegation] alone shall not constitute *prima facie* evidence of discrimination nor shall it shift the burden of proof to the challenged party'. In short, failure to meet quotas would not, as in 1972, constitute proof of racial discrimination.

This proposed shift away from quotas was greeted with great hostility by various groups within the party, particularly the caucuses of blacks and militant feminists. A crucial meeting was held between them and Robert Strauss, and he agreed to the deletion of the explicit repudiation of quotas.[33] It is important to be clear that Strauss did not agree, nor did the Convention, to an explicit affirmation that quotas would be imposed in 1976. However, he did agree to maintain a highly ambiguous situation in which quotas might or might not be enforced. The compromise on ambiguity was accepted by the Democratic Governors (indeed, it was moved on the floor by Reubin Askew, Governor of Florida) and by Mayor Daley, who uttered the memorable statement, 'I recognize when power shifts.' It was not accepted by Barkan or Meany. Barkan lost his attack on quotas massively, winning only two out of forty-four votes on the Rules Committee of the Convention and forcing Barkan to recognise that 'we don't have the votes'[34] to change the proposed charter. Barkan and Meany lapsed once more into a sullen bitterness. Meany himself was so angry with Strauss for compromising on quotas that he refused to talk to him or return his telephone calls.[35] Alan Baron, who worked first for Senator Muskie and then for Senator McGovern, argued for once with justice that 'If you take that stereotype of the old McGovernite – the picture of an ideological purist who wanted to take over the Democratic Party and purge the other side – Al Barkan is the biggest McGovernite of them all.'[36]

Appropriately, the fight over quotas was symbolic rather than substantive. As he himself probably realised, Mayor Daley could fill his delegation with blacks, women or the young without any serious consequences following. Yet the symbolism, and the AFL-CIO's defeat was important. Meany and Barkan had tried hard to re-shape the Democratic Party and had lost. Why?

The first reason for their defeat was that the Democratic Party had changed since they had left it to sulk in 1969. The party had always been a coalition of regional interests and ideologies. After 1968, however, two groups had become established for the first time. The feminist movement established a vociferous presence and caucus. More importantly, because the vote they represented was increasingly important to the party, so did the blacks.[37] In the old days, labour had been the only interest group of consequence inside the Democratic Party. Ironically, and perhaps justly, during the time that Meany and Barkan had refused to participate in its affairs, the Democratic Party had seen the arrival of new interests. Now labour was but one of several interest groups operating openly inside the party.

Moreover, in many ways labour was now the least organised interest group within the party itself. One of the most striking features of the Kansas City convention was the loss of control over labour delegates by Meany and Barkan. The *New York Times* commented that 'Alexander E. Barkan, a presence in Democratic politics since the Depression [something of an exaggeration] has all but officially been dethroned as broker of labour power inside the Democratic Party.'[38] Of course, there never has been any real chance that those delegates whom the United Auto Workers had helped elect would be prepared to take orders from George Meany. More significant, however, was the refusal of many of the unions within the AFL-CIO to take his orders either.

By and large, these unions were those which had been particularly outraged by the decision to stay neutral in the 1972 election. The most visible of these at the convention were the Communications Workers and AFSCME. These, and delegates linked to the IAM, Oil, Chemical and Atomic Workers, Union of Electricians, Graphic Arts International Union, found themselves operating more closely with the UAW than with Barkan or Meany. This *ad hoc* caucus of liberal unions found that it could play a crucial part in the convention. Ironically, one of the first examples of their importance, unwelcome though it was to Meany, was in persuading the Democratic Governors to retreat from their initial commitment to the total abolition of quotas and to accept the Strauss compromise on ambiguity.[39] The 'liberal labour coalition' was far from a rump. Though nominally representing only a minority of labour unions, observers thought that in practice it controlled the votes of over half the delegates to the Convention linked to labour unions.[40] Not only did Barkan and Meany's extremism prompt a split within the ranks of organised labour; they themselves seemed to be on the losing side.

The emergence of the liberal union caucus placed Meany in great difficulties. The caucus became more institutionalised as the 1976 election drew nearer, and by 1976 was appearing as the Labor Coalition Clearinghouse.[41] Its members were six AFL-CIO unions – the Communications Workers, IAM, AFSCME, Oil, Chemical and Atomic Workers, Graphic Arts International Union and Union of Electricians—and three unions not in the AFL-CIO, the UAW, United Mine Workers and the National Educational Association which was being rapidly 'politicised' by Republican vetoes of bills on education. Unable to agree on the virtues of any single candidate for the Democratic nomination, the Labor Coalition was united by three beliefs. The first was that the new system of delegate selection could benefit labour unions because unions could, in fact, mobilise members to turn out in elections. The second was that it was extremely likely that the Democratic Convention would be deadlocked. This belief was entirely reasonable as the 1976 delegate selection process would for the first time operate entirely on the basis of the proportional allocation of delegates in terms of votes won; the principle of 'winner take all', giving the candidate with the most votes, even if less than 50 per cent, all a state's delegates, had been abolished. As there was a large number of contenders, it seemed unlikely that anyone would win a majority. At a deadlocked convention, the Labor Coalition believed that the 500 delegates from labour unions it had elected, nominally supporting a range of candidates, would be crucial. Third, the Labor Coalition believed it essential to ensure that the Democratic nominee would not, like McGovern, have to fight without effective labour support. In 1972, most of the unions in the Labor Coalition had rallied to McGovern's cause, but deprived of COPE's organisation, lacked the machinery to support him effectively. By 1976, as we have seen in chapter 2, the unions in the Coalition had developed an electoral capacity independent of COPE. If Meany again stayed neutral, the Coalition would coordinate their work for the Democratic candidate. In short, the Labour Coalition unions unambiguously placed themselves in the Democratic Party.

What of Meany? The attempt to discover a viable bipartisan strategy had continued throughout 1974. In that year some very unusually liberal Republicans, Schweiker (Pennsylvania), Javits (New York) and Mathias (Maryland), had been endorsed by COPE, partly because their liberal record justified it, and partly because the AFL-CIO wished to put pressure on the Democrats. Yet COPE remained tied to the Democrats. The *Congressional Quarterly* noted that the AFL-CIO was cheered by the successes of the Democrats in the 1972 congressional elections. Hathaway's victory in Maine and Abourezk's in South Dakota brought particular pleasure.[42] Very few Republicans – other than those mentioned – were worthy of COPE's support in 1974. More typical of COPE's efforts than its backing for Schweiker in Pennsylvania was its strenuous support for the Democratic challenger for one of the New Hampshire Senate seats, Durkin, in the mid-term election and the special election ordered when the Senate was unable to agree on who had won the desperately close initial contest.

As time passed, Meany's determination to boycott the Democratic Party in presidential contests looked less viable for both internal and external political reasons. In 1972, he had been able to pretend plausibly that he could not act to support McGovern for fear of a revolt by right wing unions. Now he was faced with an organised revolt by the Labor Coalition unions committed to the Democratic Party. Victor Gotbaum, second most powerful man in the AFSCME, had taken to attacking publicly the 'rightist leadership' of the AFL-CIO;[43] if Meany stayed neutral again, other unions might join the Labor Coalition creating a *de facto* split in the labour movement similar to that ended by the merger of the AFL and CIO in 1955. Moreover, it became ever clearer that Republican Presidents were unlikely to fulfil labour's objectives. The AFL-CIO's submission to the Democratic platform committee had been far from conservative. Its demands were full employment, tax reform, an attack on poverty, National Health Insurance, action on pollution, a housing programme, better schools, a measure to prevent 'the export of jobs' through tax allowances for multi-national companies and civil rights measures other than those based on quotas.[44] After initial interest in the idea of a guaranteed minimum income, Nixon looked unlikely to meet any of these demands.

Indeed, in a number of vital respects, first Nixon, and then Ford, proved ever less acceptable to labour unions. The first of these was employment. The world recession of the mid-1970s did not spare the United States. Unemployment in 1975 reached 11.7 per cent for blue collar workers, and 8.3 per cent for craft workers. In 1976, unemployment reached 17.6 per cent for construction workers. There was a national average unemployment of 7.5 per cent in 1975 and 7.9 per cent in 1976. The AFL-CIO pointed out that these rates were based on calculations which included only those who had recently looked for a job and not those who had given up in despair. It put forward as a more realistic national figure for those unemployed: 11.5 per cent in August 1975 and 10.5 per cent in August 1976.[45] In the view of the AFL-CIO the Nixon and Ford Administrations were insufficiently concerned with the issue. Nixon did little through increased public spending to combat the recession; Ford in fact used the veto vigorously to keep public spending down, believing (like Hoover) that the best recovery would spring spontaneously from the private sector. In the battle against unemployment, the AFL-CIO found natural allies among the groups representing blacks and other minorities who suffer perpetually higher rates of unemployment than the national average. It received no encouragement from the Republican Presidents.

The poor performance of Nixon and Ford in terms of the AFL-CIO's general economic measures might conceivably have been matched by concessions to the AFL-CIO elsewhere. It was not. Far from gratifying Meany's hawkish instincts, the Nixon and Ford administrations were distinctly doveish. Ford inherited a Vietnam policy from Nixon which extricated the United States from Vietnam but did not prevent the collapse of the government of South Vietnam. Moreover, under the guidance of Henry Kissinger, as Secretary of State, detente was pursued vigorously to the dismay of the AFL-CIO. In order to avoid offending the Russians, Ford refused to receive prominent Russian dissidents such as Solzhenitsyn at the White House. But the AFL-CIO feted Solzhenitsyn at a special reception. Moreover, other policies seemed to indicate that the Nixon and Ford Administrations imposed the costs on labour unions which they have learnt to fear from Republican administrations. Most obviously, as well as labor unions, the 'Nixon Court' turned out to be less than well disposed towards civil libertarians or the NAACP (National Association for the Advancement of Colored People). Most notable of a number of cases decided in way unwelcome to the AFL-CIO was a ruling that the Congress had no constitutional power to impose minimum wage rates on city or state governments.[46] The public sector unions which had hoped to extend their industrial power by political means were not pleased. Nor were the maritime unions when President Ford vetoed a bill they had understood he would sign that would have increased the proportion of oil imports carried in American ships.

Perhaps the most vivid single instance seeming to indicate that Republicans would always be anti-union was over 'situs picketing'. As part of a general review of law affecting industrial relations in the construction industry, the Secretary of Labour, John Dunlop, had publicly accepted that construction unions should be allowed to picket a whole site, not just one employer on it. This legalisation of 'common situs picketing' would void the prohibition on secondary boycotts (e.g. carpenters striking in support of plumbers) that was contained in the general labour law. Dunlop, an academic expert on labour unions, was likely to be sympathetic. However, he ensured that he had the support of President Ford. Ford's election strategy would have been well served by such a move; Ford needed to conciliate the construction unions as they are the most conservative of the unions. Unfortunately, the strategy Ford was compelled to follow in the primaries was not in line with the best strategy for November. Hard pressed by an extreme right winger, the former Governor of California, Ronald Reagan, Ford felt that he could not afford to appear 'pro-union' in a competition for the support of conservative Republican primary voters. Accordingly, he vetoed the bill, prompting the resignation of John Dunlop and the wrath of the conservative construction unions. Not even the conservative unions would oppose supporting the Democrats in 1976.

In short, by 1976 it had become obvious that Republican Presidents were likely to do little for labour. Meany had rather boxed himself in. In 1974, the AFL-CIO had broken with Nixon and had joined the call for his impeachment. Yet the events at Kansas City prompted a further change of strategy. AFL-CIO officials were once more ordered to cease active participation in the Democratic Party, thus reversing a policy decision taken in 1973 to enter the party in order to drive out the McGovernites. This policy was itself partially reversed in 1976, when the AFL-CIO made a belated attempt to win the Pennsylvania primary for Senator Jackson, who approached its ideals by combining a liberal domestic record with a 'hawkish' line on foreign policy. As the effort was too late and, in the absence of help from the unions in the Labor Coalition, too little, the intervention was completely unsuccessful, even amongst blue collar workers; Jackson was forced to bow out of the race for the nomination.

Thus during 1976, Meany found himself in a totally unsatisfactory position. On the one hand, it was clear that any repeat of the 1972 decision to stay neutral would prompt a serious split inside the labour movement, particularly as the liberal unions were prepared this time to support a Democrat. Indeed, the record of Nixon and Ford made it clear that almost any Democrat would be an improvement on them. On the other hand, Meany had ordered an end to active participation in the Democratic Party, and decided that the AFL-CIO would await the selection of the Democratic and Republican nominees before deciding whom to endorse. In short, Meany reverted to a pure form of Gompersism, awaiting developments in each party before making a commitment.

However, times had changed since Gompers was President of the AFL. Far from there being a free and unfettered choice between the competing parties, Meany was faced with one party, the Republicans, whose front-runner, Ford, was proven unsatisfactory, and whose main challenger, Reagan, was even worse, while Meany had foresworn participation, and hence influence, in the party which was his best hope, the Democrats. The AFL-CIO sat on the sidelines while its favourites – Jackson, Humphrey and Bayh – made no progress. Instead a Southerner, Jimmy Carter, who might easily have been anti-union (but was not) stormed through, challenged most effectively by Mo Udall of Arizona, whom the AFL-CIO suspected of McGovernism. Even worse, the isolation of the AFL-CIO from the Democrats meant that the real representatives of labour to the main contenders became the officials of the Labor Coalition. Indeed, one of its officials, Bill Holayter of the IAM was named as the labour liaison official for the Carter campaign.

In this situation, the best that Meany could do was to rush to endorse Carter as soon as he received the Democratic nomination and to offer him COPE's support. The initial plan had been for the AFL-CIO Executive Council to hold a special meeting after both party conventions in August. In the event, the Council held its meeting in July before the Republicans even met at Kansas City, and endorsed Carter. The fact that Carter was generally considered at this stage an unknown outsider whose position on issues was said to be vague, emphasised how little freedom of action the AFL-CIO had. Meany had been forced to accept any reasonable candidate the Democratic Party produced though the AFL-CIO had played no real part in the process, and had been powerless to affect its outcome. Only the high value which Carter placed on the power of the AFL-CIO's Committee on Political Education to help him become President saved the situation. Eager for such support in a campaign which was noticeably short of money, Carter was prepared to court Meany and the AFL-CIO in public and in private, even though this meant rescinding the promises made to the Labor Coalition. This never went so far as to leave Carter prepared to identify himself as the AFL-CIO's candidate, for 'special interests' were out of fashion in the 1976 election. It was enough, however, to end Carter's reliance on the Labor Coalition as sole or pre-eminent spokesman for the unions.

CONCLUSIONS: LABOUR AND THE DEMOCRATIC PARTY

Part of the American labour movement, broadly speaking those unions who affiliated to the Labor Coalition, has resolved permanently the ambiguity of its relationship with the Democratic Party. They participate in its primaries, seek to ensure they have a significant number of delegates at its conventions, and are in some degree morally bound to accept the platform and candidate produced by the process in which they are involved. These unions, barring some cataclysmic shift in American politics, have joined the Democratic Party. Another group of unions, within the AFL-CIO, is not that far away. Every instinct bar one pulls the American Federation of Teachers (AFT), and the International Ladies Garment Workers' Union (ILGWU) towards the

Democrats; the sole exception is loyalty to the AFL-CIO's leadership. Another group, the maritime unions and the construction unions, will never be interested in politics except for instrumental purposes.

What of the remainder, probably still the majority and the AFL-CIO itself? There is little doubt that in congressional elections, the AFL-CIO will continue to endorse predominantly Democrats with the odd exception, such as Schweiker, serving only to emphasise the distance between organised labour and the average conservative Republican. Presidential elections will continue to cause the most difficulty. Recent events seem to suggest that the interests of organised labour as the AFL-CIO perceives them, will be better served by Democratic rather than Republican Presidents. It is more or less agreed amongst the political activists in organised labour that the unions paid a price for Nixon's victories. The low priority attached by the Nixon and Ford Administrations to reducing unemployment and the 'anti-union' attitudes evinced by the decisions of Nixon's nominees to the Supreme Court are the most obvious examples. At present, the view amongst the AFL-CIO staff is that self-interest suggests that unions side with the Democrats, a view which we shall see in chapter 5 is justified. Writing just before the 1976 elections in the AFL-CIO's official journal, its associate editor, Rex Hardesty, noted that Carter and Mondale

> . . . still faced many pitfalls, most of which fit the mould of lifestyle v. pocketbook which have left Democrats winning only two of the last six presidential elections. Nixon couldn't have won and touched off the conservative resurgence of 1968 without the lifestyle issues and war in South East Asia. The Nixon White House worked up a credo [sic crescendo?] tuned to fear of abrupt change and popularised it with slogans of the three a's of anarchy, abortion and acid for use against George McGovern in 1972.[47]

The writer did not need, perhaps, to point out that Meany was one of those who bought the product.

Yet if the AFL-CIO has been forced to accept the folly of its flirtation with Republicans such as Nixon, it has not come to terms with how to participate in the party. On the one hand, the total lack of influence it enjoyed in 1976 over the selection of the Democratic nominee is clearly unsatisfactory. On the other hand, the alternative strategies also contain risks and perils. The most obvious of these is the fear held in COPE circles, and triumphantly repeated by spokesmen for the new liberals, that COPE cannot participate successfully in primaries. This fear (or hope) is, of course, unproven – COPE has yet to make a sustained attempt to win the nomination for one of its favourites. Like the campaigns of the 'old liberals' such as Muskie, Jackson and Humphrey it has supported, COPE's forays into primaries have been belated and half hearted. Yet there is no reason to suppose that COPE's organisation could not function in a primary. It is true that the voters whom it mobilises, being of lower socio-economic status, are less likely to participate in primaries spontaneously. Yet Jimmy Carter was highly dependent in his brilliantly successful primary campaign on the support of blacks. Moreover, the most obvious rivals to COPE, the student and peace movements of the 1960s, have faded. Were COPE to back one candidate throughout primary election campaigns, it would face fewer organised rivals today than in the era of the Vietnam War. A participatory selection process in general favours an organisation like COPE with money, organisation, skill and numerous followers.

There are, however, less obvious problems. In the first place, a strategy which relied upon open and sustained participation in the Democratic primaries would mark an end to the pretence at bipartisan political activity, a formal end to the Gompers tradition. Whether the aged leadership at present in control of the AFL-CIO is capable of making such a break with tradition is highly questionable. Nor are the barriers in the way of such a change merely those of senility or stupidity. One feature of contests for the Democratic nomination is that they are frequently fought between people who have much in common. Carter, Bayh, Humphrey, Udall, Jackson and even Brown of California, the main runners of 1976, were all reasonably close on *domestic* issues. This, far from being an entirely desirable state of affairs, would, in fact, cause the AFL-CIO problems if it wishes to participate in Democratic primaries. In the first place, it would have to back one of its established friends in preference to the others. For example, if the AFL-CIO had to make a sustained effort to help Jackson in 1976, Udall, Bayh and Humphrey could feel justly that they had received scant reward for years of loyalty to the causes which the AFL-CIO supports. Even more awkwardly, the unions affiliated to the AFL-CIO would be no more likely to agree on one person as the choice for Democratic nominee than would the British affiliates of the TUC on the choice of leader of the Labour Party or Prime Minister of a Labour Government. Indeed, just as the General and Municipal Workers' in Britain would prefer a right wing member of the Parliamentary Labour Party and the President of the Association of Scientific, Technical and Managerial Staff a Tribunite, so in the United States the ILGWU would prefer an old-style liberal and the AFSCME someone from the new liberals. Participation by the AFL-CIO in the nomination process would produce sharp divisions precisely because the difference between the candidates is so narrow.

It must be admitted, therefore, that the current Democratic nominating process is unsuited to the AFL-CIO, not so much because it is participatory but because it is protracted and public. We may note that the Labor Coalition, which is more politically homogeneous than the AFL-CIO itself, was still incapable of agreeing on a single candidate for the Democratic nomination in 1976. Instead, it supported all the reasonably liberal contenders (including Jackson and Carter) who would place union people in the lists of delegates to the Convention. All this was done in the hope of influencing a deadlocked Convention which never happened. Whether, had the Convention been deadlocked, the Labor Coalition could have agreed on one candidate to whom it could have delivered the votes of all the delegates affiliated to it is very doubtful. The AFL-CIO would find any decision on backing only one contender immeasurably more difficult than did the Labor Coalition. Yet, equally, the strategy of waiting for the party to make a choice and then endorsing it (or not) is not one which maximises labour's influence either. Both in 1972 and 1976 the Democratic Party chose a nominee who was far from being the AFL-CIO's first choice. In 1976, the organisation felt that it could (or would have to) live with the decision. In 1972 it did not. In the future, the leaders of the AFL-CIO must surely try to find a way in which they can participate in the Democratic Party in a way which brings home to the party the importance of its working class following. The continued ambiguity in the AFL-CIO's attitude to the Democratic Party is a self-inflicted cut in the political power of organised labour.

4 Labour's Lobbyists

In previous chapters, we began to accumulate evidence that the absence of a Labour Party in the United States has not resulted (as is so often supposed) in the insulation of unions from politics. On the contrary, unions have been forced to realise that if politicians are to be elected who are sympathetic to the interests and aspirations of unions, they must do something to influence the outcome of elections themselves. Of course, as any realistic observer of politics will know, there is often a gap between promises made by candidates during election campaigns and their performance thereafter. This gap, and the complex legislative process in the United States, makes it necessary for unions to employ lobbyists to urge the adoption of legislation they favour and the rejection of legislation they oppose; intervening in elections alone is insufficient. In this chapter we shall examine how these lobbyists work. We shall evaluate their effectiveness and discuss what political objectives are pursued by organised labour's lobbyists. A further obvious question is what relationship exists between the electoral activities of the unions and COPE in particular and the work of the lobbyists employed by organised labour. It is uncertain how closely these activities are linked and how dependent the lobbyists are for their success or influence on the threat that COPE might pose to a legislator's chances of re-election.

LOBBYING: THE GENERAL CONTEXT

Lobbying has always attracted much attention in discussions of American politics. The old picture of a lobbyist was of an unscrupulous operator paying cash for congressional votes or favours. Contrary to the belief expressed in most text books, this sort of activity has not ceased. The Government of South Korea and sophisticated modern corporations such as ITT both allegedly have tried to make their arguments more convincing by dispensing cash or services. Yet standard texts probably are correct in asserting that this underhand

57

variant of lobbying is less important than the open operations of political technicians who seek to persuade legislators through powers of argument, at worst buttressed with campaign contributions or references to blocks of votes. For some, lobbying is the practical expression of American pluralism, a political system which offers every interest a chance to influence decisions. Such optimistic assessments of the workings of pluralist systems became less common in the 1960s as American radicals noted that not all interests were organised and had lobbyists, and that prevailing attitudes favoured some and handicapped others. More significantly for our purposes, empirical studies suggested that the importance of lobbyists was overstated. The largest study of American lobbyists[1] concluded that they were relatively weak, a conclusion supported by other studies. Lobbyists were too slow to contact wavering congressmen, left others in the dark about their attitudes, talked only to legislators who were already converted, and were underfinanced and ill-informed.

Labour lobbyists might not fit this general picture. Not only might labour lobbyists be more efficient than most but the electoral capability of labour, which we encountered in the first chapter, might provide them with a power that most lobbyists lack.

LABOUR LOBBYISTS AT WORK

Every international union has a Washington lobbyist; several maintain two or three. The labour lobbyists who attract the most attention on Capitol Hill are not these, however, but the seven full-time lobbyists employed by the AFL-CIO itself. Of course, these two groups are neither isolated nor finite. The usual understanding between individual unions and the AFL-CIO is that the primary initiative on general issues is left to the AFL-CIO lobbyists, but the other lobbyists are happy to assist when called upon for help. In a major drive, the seven AFL-CIO lobbyists can be increased to over 50 by mobilising other union lobbyists based in Washington. This understanding is not a rigid demarcation, however. The United Auto Workers, which left the AFL-CIO in 1967, may cooperate with the AFL-CIO in working on many issues such as national health insurance, but would not concede any primacy to it. Individual unions within the AFL-CIO with particularly capable lobbyists, such as the ILGWU, will take the opportunity presented by their links with senators or congressmen to press for legislation of wide significance. The IAM, the Meatcutters and the American Federation of State, County and Municipal Employees (AFSCME) are other examples of unions within the AFL-CIO which have active lobbyists who work regularly on issues other than those of immediate concern to their union.

Labour lobbyists also benefit from the support of union officials. From time to time these union officials may lobby representatives and senators at the request of the regular lobbyists, by contacting the legislators either in Washington, or in the district or state.

After all these caveats have been stated, we can say that the labour lobbyists are primarily the lobbyists of the AFL-CIO. It is they who, in terms of numbers, contacts and attention to general issues, dominate the labour lobbying scene. They are closely supported by the politically liberal unions inside and outside the AFL-CIO (particularly the UAW), while the more narrowly focused craft unions and Teamsters are less active and well known. Though the craft unions and Teamsters account for a substantial proportion of union membership in the United States, the labour lobbyists whom congressmen and senators know best will be those from the AFL-CIO, followed by those from the liberal, politically active unions. To a greater degree than their membership figures might suggest, most lobbying by unions in the United States is carried out by liberal unions; conservative unions tend to be inactive.

The AFL-CIO lobbyists have earned a reputation for skill and effectiveness. Congressmen, whether or not they agree with its policies, refer to the AFL-CIO as 'the best lobby on the Hill'.[2] What constitutes this excellence requires closer examination. The favourable assessment of the AFL-CIO as a lobby reveals much about the skills that a good lobbyist requires. First, the AFL-CIO lobbyists have a thorough knowledge of Congress. This means that they know congressional procedures extremely well. AFL-CIO lobbyists know the tactical traps awaiting a bill, and the best ways in which to ensure the bill's escape or its snaring. Knowledge of Congress has a political element too. That aspect is knowledge of who already favours a proposal, who opposes, and who is wavering. The labour lobbyists, with their close daily contact, have a knowledge of congressional opinion on a wide variety of issues, and are likely to know too what concessions on other issues or on this particular proposal are necessary to secure a majority. In short, the detailed knowledge of congressional opinion enables the AFL-CIO to help build winning coalitions on a wide variety of issues.

The political knowledge of the AFL-CIO lobbyists is supplemented by a reputation for being well-briefed and informed on the substantive details of the issues they are handling. This is, of course, only to be expected given the resources available through the AFL-CIO's lavishly funded and equipped headquarters. (The AFL-CIO's budget is about six times as high as the British TUC's.) Nevertheless, reliable technical advice is something which congressmen naturally prize. When this reputation for being well informed about the specific issue is added to the reputation for being well informed about the balance of congressional opinion and the procedural risks a bill faces, the value of guidance from the AFL-CIO lobbyists to a legislator is obvious, so long as he or she trusts this guidance. The busy congressman or senator can be given a speedy summary of all the technical and political information he needs in a session with the AFL-CIO lobbyists, and he often will regard this information as fully trustworthy.

LABOUR LOBBYING TACTICS

The AFL-CIO lobbyists have put considerable emphasis on developing a trusting relationship between themselves and members of Congress. They are likely to warn legislators of the technical or political problems implicit in a proposal they are supporting instead of disguising its disadvantages. The development of a close and trusting relationship implies following a 'soft sell' approach. The most visible of the senior AFL-CIO lobbyists today is Ken Young. A study by the prestigious *Congressional Quarterly* captured Young's style by quoting a Senate Committee aide:

> He's very soft spoken, soft sell; he knows his facts. If you've got a question, he's got an answer for it. He doesn't threaten, he doesn't cajole; he doesn't plead. But he won't take 'no' for an answer . . . The AFL-CIO legislative department is marked by professionalism. They rarely come in heavy handed.[3]

The soft sell approach has a number of implications. The most important is that the electoral capacity of labour is not emphasised as a punishment or reward. A rapid recourse to threats of electoral retribution would complicate day to day working relationships with congressmen and senators whose votes may be needed in the future. Moreover, many congressmen and senators, particularly Southern Democrats, whose votes on an issue may well be crucial, would only benefit electorally from being marked down as an enemy of labour unions. Gentle persuasion may be more successful and, indeed, the only practical strategy.

Yet though AFL-CIO lobbyists rarely like to remind legislators of their political power, it would be naive to assume that legislators are unaware that it is there. Indeed two *Washington Post* reporters found that 'Labor is not only competent and powerful. It is feared.'[4] A congressman from a non-Southern district may not be vulnerable to attack from labour alone, but he or she would surely be aware that his next primary or election could be made more difficult by the intervention of COPE with the resources we described in chapter 2. That tactful AFL-CIO lobbyists choose not to remind a congressman of this power is immaterial; he knows that it is there. Indeed, it could be argued that some standard AFL-CIO lobbying techniques are, in fact, subtle reminders of this power. These techniques include the common ploy of encouraging union members or officials who are a legislator's constituents to contact him to reinforce the message from the professional lobbyist. Even Senator Russell Long (Democrat Louisiana), has been reminded that union power extends into his constituency though it has not swayed him often, particularly on tax reform.[5] During the campaign for Medicare, Senator Ribicoff (Democrat, Connecticut), complained to an AFL-CIO lobbyist about a flood of telegrams from his state inspired by the unions. The lobbyist replied, 'You know and I know, Abe, that if I come in here and you had not got all these wires, you wouldn't pay much attention to me.' The lobbyist was exaggerating, but he had a point.[6]

Perhaps the most fundamental reason why labour lobbyists follow a 'soft sell' strategy is that, as we have seen in chapter 1, unions in the United States are a perpetual minority. Even if labour could deploy electorally all its members, it would be deploying no more than 28 per cent of the non-agricultural workforce. Though COPE extends labour's powers beyond this, unions in the United States are doomed to coalition politics, and the lobbying tactics of the AFL-CIO rest on this. Ken Young has commented that 'We do best when we are part of a coalition.'[7] AFL-CIO lobbyists seek alliances with others who enjoy close relations with the legislators with whom the unions are not on close terms. One of the oldest alliances the AFL-CIO has is with the National Farmers' Union, a liberal farm group. As the Black Caucus in Congress increases in strength, the AFL-CIO is finding that its long-standing and principled support for civil rights legislation has a practical pay-off as civil rights groups whip in votes which unions themselves might not easily mobilise. One of the most striking examples of such groups helping unions was in 1965. Liberal groups which the AFL-CIO had long aided helped it rally votes for repeal of Section 14(b) of the Taft-Hartley Act which allows states to enact 'right to work' laws. The National Association for the Advancement of Colored People (NAACP), the Americans for Democratic Action (ADA), the National Farmer's Union (NFU) and, even more surprisingly, the National Council of Churches, all testified in favour of the repeal of the clause which unions of all sorts have long opposed.[8]

In all the alliances mentioned so far, the AFL-CIO is by far the stronger partner. In terms of political muscle, the AFL-CIO stands in relation to the NAACP as, for example, the United States does to Norway in terms of military power within NATO. Yet it has not always been like this, there being one major exception. During the Kennedy and Johnson Administrations, careful contact on at least a weekly basis was maintained between the White House and Meany and between the chief AFL-CIO lobbyist, Andrew Biemiller, and the head of White House legislative liaison, Larry O'Brien.[9] These meetings were to coordinate strategy in lobbying for the 'Great Society' and other liberal legislation. Only in this relationship did the AFL-CIO find itself working with a more powerful partner.

Two departures from the pattern of 'restrained competence' should be noted. The first concerns unions within the AFL-CIO and the second is the behaviour of the AFL-CIO itself on 'labour' issues.

Unions within the AFL-CIO usually follow the practices of the umbrella organisation's officers. There are occasions when they do not. Indeed, some of the compliments paid to the AFL-CIO lobbyists quoted above were made in the context of critical comments about individual unions. Thus the Senate source who told the *Congressional Quarterly* that the AFL-CIO's lobbyists 'rarely come in heavy handed' added: 'That's not true of individual unions. You get the legislative directors of the unions calling up and saying that they will withdraw their money in the next election.'[10] An oft-quoted example of the rougher style of labour politics are the Maritime Unions. Indeed, the opposition of the Maritime Unions to the re-organisation of the House Committee system, proposed by the Bolling Committee, was due to their reluctance to see the House Merchant Marine and Fisheries Committee disturbed. The Maritime Unions had bought members of the Committee several times over with campaign contributions and were naturally reluctant to lose their investment. The Maritime Unions have been very effective in netting large subsidies for the American merchant fleet. The AFL-CIO itself is after somewhat bigger fish, and it would be erroneous to assume that it could succeed through such tactics.

The other exception to the picture of the labour lobbyists as restrained but effective professionals comes, surprisingly, from the field of labour relations law. The track record of the labour unions on labour legislation is, despite their general reputation, dismal. Labour has often been successful in working for general measures; it has usually been defeated on specifically labour issues. The passage of the Taft-Hartley Act in 1947, which seriously curtailed the rights of labour unions, may be explained easily as it occurred before the AFL-CIO had merged or its member unions developed a significant political capability. The enactment of the Landrum-Griffin Act in 1959 (The Labor Management Reporting and Disclosure Act) was also a reverse for unions, though the version of the bill adopted was much less damaging than had seemed likely.

Labour lobbyists themselves see the answer in terms of the absence of a friendly coalition on the issue. Ken Young has argued that 'You don't have a coalition on a pure labour issue.'[11] Representative Abner Mikva (D., Illinois) has echoed this view. 'They've [the labour lobbyists] never been able to make [repeal of] Section 14(b) [of the Taft-Hartley Act] an issue to Common Cause or the Committee for an Effective Congress or even to the Americans for Democratic Action.'[12] In one sense, they are right. Liberal sentiment in the United States does not sympathise with unions now as it did instinctively before the 1950s. Yet in terms of lobbying both were over-stating the case. As we have seen, the AFL-CIO does have liberal friends, including the ADA, who have supported repeal. That new liberal groups such as Common Cause are not interested in such issues has a significance to which we shall return; to suggest that all liberals are indifferent to labour issues is to do violence to the facts. The limited success that labour lobbyists have enjoyed in repealing Taft-Hartley is most probably due to the advantage which congressional procedure gives to the *status quo*. After all, repeal of the most disliked part of Taft-Hartley, 14(b), passed the House of Representatives in 1965 and would have been approved by President Johnson. The measure was the victim of a Senate filibuster which the AFL-CIO could not override with the requisite two-thirds majority.

It is less easy to explain why the unions lost control of events during the passage of Landrum-Griffin, in spite of the help provided by one of the best case studies in American politics on the measure. As the author of that study, McAdams,[13] points out, the unions enjoyed numerous advantages on paper during this period. The 1958 mid-term elections had been a landslide victory for the Democrats, a landslide which had brought to Congress a clear liberal majority, well disposed to the AFL-CIO. The 'conservative coalition' of Republicans and conservative Southern Democrats lost control of the Education and Labor Committee. The fact that Congress came close to passing a version of Landrum-Griffin which would have handicapped unions significantly can be understood only by recalling the power of 'union corruption' as an issue at the time following the disgraceful abuses which the McClellan Committee discovered in a small minority of unions. Prompted by President Eisenhower, strong public opinion on the issue made some legislation inevitable. Yet as the AFL-CIO itself was engaged in a drive against corruption itself – a drive culminated in the expulsion of the Teamsters – such legislation need not have posed a threat to the industrial power of unions. That such a threat was embodied in the version of the bill which passed the House was due to gross political miscalculation by the labour unions, a miscalculation which turned on the assumption that the liberal Democratic majority would prevent any labour legislation being passed. The AFL-CIO lobbyists therefore opposed the passage of any labour legislation at all. How can such a miscalculation be squared with the argument that labour lobbyists who were warned of the dangers by Democratic Party leaders in Congress, are skilled and effective?

The key to the problem is that the labour lobbyists were not deciding strategy on this issue. Whereas labour lobbyists are allowed considerable autonomy in deciding tactics on issues such as national health insurance, civil rights, on hard labour issues the actual leaders of the AFL-CIO take over. We shall see how this affected congressional reform proposals in the 1970s; in the case of Landrum-Griffin, Meany's semi-official biographer tells us that Meany himself took control of strategy.[14] The mistakes which were made were not mistakes made by the regular lobbyists but by the more powerful but more remote leaders of the organisation who insisted on handling tactics on this issue themselves.

It is only fair to add that since 1959 labour lobbyists have prevented the passage of any legislation which is inimical to the interests of labour. This has been achieved through close cooperation with the Democratic Party leaders who have taken care that all appointees to the House Education and Labor Committee or the Senate Labor and Public Welfare Committee are sympathetic to the unions. Indeed, in the case of the Senate Committee, not only the Democrats are sympathetic to the unions; to the dismay of their House colleagues[15] several of the

Republicans on the Committee are such unusually liberal and pro-union Republicans as Javits (New York)[16] and Schweiker (Pennsylvania). Labour lobbyists, who have extremely close relations with such liberal Republicans and Democrats can rely on them to kill any anti-union legislation in Committee. Indeed, in the House Committee, where practically all the member Republicans are regarded as anti-union, the Republicans complain that labour legislation is written in caucuses of labour lobbyists and the Democrats. Indeed, it is not uncommon for the Committee to be adjourned so that the Democrats can clarify the views of labour union lobbyists on points which have arisen in debate. The Democrats then return to Committee and vote through the text agreed with union lobbyists.[17] Thus since 1959, the labour lobbyists, using their expertise and close ties to the liberals in Congress (who are usually Democrats) have been able to avoid any further erosion of the legal position of unions in the United States.

WHAT DO LABOUR LOBBYISTS DO?

There are many occasions when labour lobbyists are concerned with legislation governing industrial relations, conditions of employment and safety at work. These issues we may term 'labour issues', and several examples have already been mentioned (though the politics of labour issues will be examined separately in a later chapter). Labour lobbyists are concerned too with issues which benefit not only union members, but many others in American society as well. For example, the state of the economy and the level of unemployment affect the bargaining position of labour unions and unemployment can hit union members as well as the unorganised. There is a third category, the extent of which we shall explore, which is not of direct concern to union members *qua* union members.

It is easy to give almost innumerable examples of our second category, measures which benefit union members but many others too. One current example is the effort the AFL-CIO is devoting to campaigning for an increase in government spending to stimulate the economy and thus reduce unemployment. This campaign has involved heavy lobbying for higher public works expenditure which would benefit unionised people such as construction workers (amongst whom unemployment reached 17 per cent in 1975). Yet many of the measures that labour has supported in order to raise public expenditure have been measures such as increasing social security payments or educational expenditure, measures whose immediate effect was to help many groups not in unions. Moreover, the first and most seriously affected victims of unemployment are not union members; they are the unskilled blacks, Puerto Ricans and ghetto dwellers who are highly marginal to the American economy. Another example of an issue which links the interest of union members *qua* union members with the interests of other Americans is national health insurance. Labour lobbyists had supported National Health Insurance (NHI) ever since President Truman called for its adoption in 1948. After the issue became one which was unlikely to be taken seriously as a political issue, strong unions such as the United Auto Workers turned to an industrial strategy in which they negotiated employer financed health insurance for themselves and their families as part of the pay contract negotiations. The current drive for NHI by labour lobbyists was started by the UAW after the Union had found that the escalating cost of health insurance had proved a major stumbling block in bargaining with the auto companies.[18] This prompted the UAW to go back to a legislative approach. Since then, NHI has been one of the AFL-CIO's and UAW's highest priorities in lobbying Congress. As in some other cases, the AFL-CIO and UAW have financed a specialist lobbying organisation focusing exclusively on NHI.

It would be easy to disparage such activity as mere self interest. To do so would be to miss two significant points. First, even if labour unions pursue goals such as NHI for no reason other than self interest, it is still of considerable importance that the self interest of labour should coincide with that of disadvantaged or Americans only averagely well-off. In some ways, such examples should cause liberal advocates of 'the new politics' particular cause for thought. Second, the pursuit of benefits for members of unions through a legislative strategy rather than through collective bargaining is of considerable importance in terms of the history of American unions. The tradition of American craft unionism associated with Samuel Gompers was one in which political action for social benefits was frowned upon. Pensions, sick pay, etc. should be secured, he argued, by unions in private schemes or by bargaining with employers both for philosophical and practical reasons; benefits linked to unions strengthened the incentive to belong and the role of the state was kept small. To the extent that the labour lobbyists have turned to legislative solutions which necessarily apply to all workers and not just the unionised minority, they have reached beyond the Gompers tradition.

There are, however, other issues which the unions, and, in particular, the AFL-CIO have pursued which stretch far beyond the interests of union members as such. One dramatic example was the statement of priorities for the new year issued by the AFL-CIO lobbyists in January 1974.

> First and foremost in the interests of national security, of preserving our democratic system of government and of restoring a fully functioning government to address the serious problems facing the nation, the impeachment of Richard Nixon.[19]

The same statement of priorities went on to list a number of other issues such as reform of the housing programme, full funding of poverty programmes, consumer protection, more funds for education and environmental protection, better veterans' programmes and the direct election of the President, all of which are of little direct relevance to union members *qua* workers. An even clearer example is civil rights legislation; American unions are often criticised because they have too few black members, yet, as we shall see, civil rights legislation has preoccupied labour lobbyists. Only a minority of American union members are likely to benefit from civil rights legislation; even fewer will benefit directly from anti-poverty legislation.

As the AFL-CIO and politically active unions work on all these categories of legislation, the important question is the balance which they strike between them. The answer varies from union to union and, to a lesser extent, according to circumstances.

It will come then as little surprise that some American unions devote themselves almost exclusively to our first category; that is, issues affecting union members as union members. Craft union lobbyists are notorious for devoting all their efforts to such issues, the most recent example being a bill to permit 'situs' (site) picketing by members of craft unions on strike. This required exempting the construction unions from the existing ban on secondary boycotts in American industrial relations law. Lobbyists from the AFL-CIO and other unions are wont to complain that though craft unions welcome their help on such an issue, they do little in return.[20] Similarly, the Teamsters do little beyond maintaining a defensive posture, avoiding any legislation or investigations which might disturb the Union's ruling group. (It is only fair to add that the Teamsters have a wider range of policy positions, however, and their lobbyists claim that they will work on them when they have a chance of adoption.)[21]

In dramatic contrast are the UAW, AFSCME and the IAM. All of these unions spend most of their time and effort on our second and third categories – measures benefiting either non-union members, as well as union members, or of no relevance to union members as such. The narrow focus of the craft unions and Teamsters has at least one major consequence. It is that the more conservative unions expend little effort on lobbying compared to the liberal unions, such as the UAW. As with electoral activity, the volume of labour lobbying is overwhelmingly liberal; the conservative unions, numerically significant though a minority, are of no consequence in terms of lobbying on issues which are more than sectional. Conservative unions may not work for many general liberal policies, but they do not work against them either.

In view of their pre-eminence amongst labour lobbyists, the major question concerns not the individual unions' lobbyists, but those from the AFL-CIO. What balance do they strike between these categories of legislation? Providing a conclusive answer to this question requires the use of a variety of evidence. One measure is the attention devoted to our categories in the AFL-CIO's lobbyists' report, *Labor looks at the . . . . . Congress.* Some recent reports give the following figures:

Topics	No. of pages per area	
	1971/2 (92nd Congress)	1973 (93rd Congress)
General economic	31	33
Labour legislation	26	19
Regarding others	74	59
Total	131	111

These randomly selected reports produce results which could be replicated in their general conclusion in any year; the AFL-CIO lobbyists claim to devote most of their efforts to causes which are not union 'interest group' legislation; indeed, they claim to spend most of their time on issues which are neither narrow union nor broad economic topics. This balance is, of course, similar to that which we observed that COPE struck in the previous chapter. It would be surprising were it to be otherwise.

Published reports by lobbyists are, of course, a suspect source. Far from accurately representing lobbyists' interests they may be dismissed as window dressing. Another approach is to interview congressmen, senators and lobbyists themselves to discover how the labour lobbyists spend their time. The results of such interviews suggest that the published reports of lobbyists are not as misleading as we might suppose. Such interviews suggest that the AFL-CIO lobbyists do, indeed, devote most of their efforts either to issues which affect labour union members, but many others too, or to issues of no direct relevance to the labour unions. One congressman, particularly close to the AFL-CIO, when asked in 1975 how often he was contacted on labour issues, replied:

> I can't remember the last time they contacted me on a pure labour issue. Was it 14(b)? [of Taft-Hartley] in 1965? No, there was one thing last year. But it's civil rights, housing, health insurance.[22]

A liberal Republican Senator endorsed by the AFL-CIO in his last election compoign agreed and attributed what he saw as labour lobbyists' effectiveness to their concentration on issues 'that benefit everyone' and not just union members. A Connecticut Democrat usually (but not always) endorsed by the AFL-CIO argued its lobbyists had 'gone way beyond labour issues', and since the 1930s had been 'the chief spokesman for the common good'. Indeed, he argued, labour lobbyists were much more effective on general rather than labour issues, when their arguments were treated with the scepticism the pleading of a special interest deserves. A New Jersey Democratic Congressman, arguably one of the AFL-CIO's favourites, asked to name the issues on which its lobbyists contacted him, replied 'almost anything', but the examples which came quickest to his mind were the Poverty Programme and voter registration legislation. A former Chief Counsel to the AFL-CIO who, as such, had been present at most of the occasions when they testified before congressional committees, found it hard to identify labour's successes because 'we've been involved in so much' but when pushed chose civil rights as the most successful field. A current AFL-CIO lobbyist, when asked what should be the legislative goals of the organisation, replied: 'If we can help the low and middle income groups in this country, that's what's good for the country. That's what we are all about.' He chose civil rights, education and the Great Society legislation as the AFL-CIO lobbyists' greatest achievements, though of course he did not claim all the credit. Another liberal Democratic Congressman, once a close ally of the AFL-CIO but of late not on terms with it because of its opposition to certain congressional reforms, was still ready to pay the AFL-CIO a generous tribute. 'Without the labour movement we wouldn't have had any of our social legislation. They were the key.'

The results of such interviews are not interesting because of the perhaps questionable (attributing too much influence to unions) analysis they contain of why certain bills became law. They are interesting because they confirm the picture of the labour lobbyist as a person who reaches beyond the sectional concerns of unions, and spends much of his time on issues of much wider significance.

One policy area, which was mentioned frequently in legislative reports and spontaneously in interviews as an area of successful union influence, was civil rights. Though many American liberals suspect unions of racism, the passage of the various civil rights and voting rights acts was the most popular nominee in interviews as the AFL-CIO's major accomplishment. It is easy to quote examples of the numerous appearances by AFL-CIO and UAW lobbyists in favour of every civil rights bill.[23] This lobbying has usually been done at the highest level with testimony from Meany as well as from the regular lobbyists and Chief Counsel. Nor has the AFL-CIO been unwilling to support unpopular measures in the civil rights area. AFL-CIO lobbyists have supported open housing legislation forbidding racial discrimination in the selling or renting of accommodation;[24] they have even opposed legislation to prohibit the bussing of school children to achieve racial integration, a technique for ending *de facto* segregation which one suspects would not find favour with all blue collar workers. Civil rights legislation has engaged AFL-CIO lobbyists more than anything else.

What happens, however, when union interests and general causes such as civil rights legislation collide? In the case of civil rights, to a surprising degree the AFL-CIO has remained true to its formal commitment to racial integration. Perhaps the most notable of the AFL-CIO's contributions to legislation in this field was its advocacy of Title VII of the Civil Rights Act of 1964. The title banned racial discrimination in personnel policies by any government agency or company receiving federal funds. The title further provided that any agency or corporation practising such discrimination should have all federal funds and grants ended forthwith. There was no doubt that when Kennedy sent his civil rights bill to Congress in 1963, he considered such a title desirable in principle. He was also sure that if he did include such a title, the whole bill would be endangered. The AFL-CIO, however, took a different view and its lobbyists worked for a title banning discrimination at the work place, as well as by governments. As Southern opponents of civil rights legislation were not slow to point out, such legislation could well be used to the disadvantage of American union members. We know that Kennedy himself asked Meany to drop the campaign for Title VII lest the whole bill fail; Meany, however, refused and appeared in person to present the AFL-CIO's arguments for the bill.[25] Lest there be any doubt about his commitment, one of Meany's exchanges with Southerners is worth quoting at length.[26]

> *Mr. Cramer*: Let me ask this. Would this section support the power of the Secretary of Labor, for instance, to cut off unemployment compensation funds or apprenticeship training funds because the Secretary essentially believes that the state or some agency of the state in the Secretary's viewpoint in its hiring practices practices discrimination?
>
> *Mr. Meany*: I want these funds cut off the same as anyone else.
>
> *Mr. Cramer*: So that the agencies that have the duty of unemployment (benefits) and others . . .
>
> *Mr. Meany*: Federal funds should be cut off.
>
> *Mr. Cramer*: Well, would you go the whole way?
>
> *Mr. Meany*: Yes.
>
> *Mr. Cramer*: Even if prejudicing the right of the unemployed laborer through unemployment compensation? This is the right of the laborer to this unemployment compensation that is being paid for by his contributions?
>
> *Mr. Meany*: That is right. He has a right to unemployment compensation but if the system is used discriminately, there should not be any funds.

It is interesting to examine why Meany took such a strong line. One reason is that he, like all top officials of the AFL-CIO, dislikes racial discrimination quite strongly. Radical critics of the labour movement often ask why Meany does not use the industrial power of unions to press for fair hiring procedures or at least insist on local unions ending their own discriminatory pressures on employers. For though there were very few, if any, unions or union locals left by the early 1960s – thanks to the efforts of the AFL-CIO – which retained explicit racialist membership rules, which had disgraced even the IAM at one stage, it was known that a significant number of locals retained racialist practices. The answer lies in the fact that, as with the TUC in Britain, the power of the AFL-CIO over constituent unions is extremely limited. By 1960, the AFL-CIO had suffered some notable set-backs in a different campaign, the attempt to end union corruption. The AFL's attempt to supplant the corrupt International Longshoremen's Association with a rival union had been rejected in a federally conducted election by a narrow but ignominious margin; the expulsion of the Teamsters had neither curtailed its growth nor weakened its leadership. Indeed, the Teamsters had gone from strength to strength while the dependence of many AFL-CIO unions on its support during strikes remained. In short, any attempt to enforce integration at their workplace by disciplining unions seemed unlikely to succeed. Meany, therefore, turned to a legislative solution. He told Congress:

> . . . we need the statutory support of the federal government to carry out the unanimously adopted principles of our own organ-ization. . . . Why is this so? Primarily because the labor movement is not what its enemies say it is – a monolithic dictatorial centralized body that imposes its will on helpless dues payers. We operate in a democratic way and cannot dictate even a good cause.[27]

It is to the credit of the AFL-CIO that it worked for civil rights legislation in general. It is interesting to note that in this case it lobbied for legislation which complicated its position as an industrial organ-isation. This is, indeed, a far cry from narrow unionism. (It is important to note, however, that Meany expressed a strong dislike for quotas on the grounds that they would handicap white workers unfairly,[28] a view which should be linked to his attitudes to quotas in the Democratic Party.)

An interesting feature of the AFL-CIO's lobbying techniques in areas such as civil rights is its financial support to specialist lobbying organisations working on the topic. Thus the AFL-CIO has paid nearly all the operating costs of the Leadership Conference on Civil Rights. Financial help has also gone to the NAACP. For example, when an Alabama judge demanded a punitive bond from the NAACP in 1975, the AFL-CIO provided over half the money, Biemiller, its legislative director, commenting that they do not desert their friends.[29] The pattern was repeated in the case of the campaign for National Health Insurance. After National Health Insurance had been pioneered by the UAW and taken up by AFL-CIO, the two organisations created the Health Security Action Council, funded by them both and headed by a former official of the UAW who was encouraged to take the job by UAW President, Leonard Woodcock. In the face of unrelenting Republican opposition, the Council developed a vigorous political action programme of its own, nearly defeating one Republican Congressman, Broyhill (N.C.) in 1974, with the imaginative slogan, 'Your Congressman may be damaging to your health.' The extra political pressure the Council has developed in favour of NHI suggests that labour's investment was worthwhile.

VARIATIONS IN LOBBYING ACTIVITIES

Though labour lobbyists remain active on a wide variety of issues, both labour lobbyists and their friends look back to the 1960s as a golden age. This is partly because relations with liberals were unclouded by disagreements over foreign policy and the structure of the Democratic Party. Vigorous lobbying by the AFL-CIO and the more political unions played a part in the adoption of Medicare, the Economic Opportunity Act, model cities, food stamps, the Trade Expansion Act and practically all the major measures that we associate with the Kennedy and Johnson years.[30] During the same period, only one serious drive for labour legislation was launched by the lobbyists, the campaign for repeal of 14(b) of Taft-Hartley. Even this campaign was timed to cause the least possible damage to efforts at enacting the Great Society legislation.[31]

To say that the Kennedy and Johnson years were a Golden Age for the labour lobbyists is not to say that the lobbyists have since abandoned the interest in social reform which they demonstrated at the time. On the contrary, in recent years there have been some striking examples of action by the AFL-CIO on general issues. Meany appeared to testify against the nomination of Clement Haynsworth to the Supreme Court, not only because his record was anti-union, but because he was indifferent to the 'legitimate aspirations of blacks'.[32] Even more interestingly, the AFL-CIO joined with its civil rights allies in campaigning against Nixon's next nominee, Carswell. 'Carswell, unlike Haynsworth, could expect an easier ride as he had no anti-union record.'[33] The Chief Counsel, Thomas Harris, told the Judiciary Committee that Carswell was wholly unacceptable.

The AFL-CIO opposes the confirmation of Judge G. Harrold Carswell as an Associate Justice of the Supreme Court. . . . We do so not because we view Judge Carswell as antagonistic to the interests of organized labour, narrowly conceived, for our view of his opinions indicates that he does not have a record of cases sufficient to permit a considered judgement. Rather the premise of our opposition is that this nomination is based exclusively on considerations of partisan political advantage and was made without consideration of professional or judicial merit.[34]

Harris defined the political motive as Nixon's 'Southern strategy' which dictated 'a relatively youthful nominee from the South, preferably a state in which the Republicans have made headway and have a good chance to make more, with a poor civil rights record and a good chance of confirmation'. Many have since argued that the successful fights against both Haynsworth and Carswell were vitally affected by the role of the AFL-CIO lobbyists.

Yet though such general issues continue to dominate the work of labour lobbyists (as we have seen above), there is something of a consensus that the lobbyists have shifted their emphasis perceptibly into general economic issues in the last few years. Why is this? The short answer is 'recession'. Unemployment in the United States has been at a postwar record high (with a reported rate over 8 per cent equivalent to a rate, calculated by the measures used in Britain, of over 10 per cent). Both COPE and the labour lobbyists have made measures which would help to reflate the economy and reduce unemployment their highest priority. As British union officials would vouch, there is nothing conservative or 'reactionary' in this. In fact, the British TUC urged the AFL-CIO to increase such efforts.[35] Of course, as many non-unionised but under-privileged groups have the highest unemployment rates, such a campaign has much to be said for it. This is not to say, however, that the legislative agenda of the labour lobbyists is influenced by the economic climate. In the cases not only of the AFL-CIO and more liberal unions, such as the UAW and AFSCME, recessions encourage greater emphasis on general economic (but not narrow union) issues. From a liberal perspective, the most creative work by labour unions is done when the economy is flourishing and 'pork chop' issues of immediate concern to their members matter least.

SETTING THE AGENDA

A question of obvious importance is how the AFL-CIO lobbyists become involved in a particular issue. Why do they devote so much time to general issues, and how are these issues selected?

In theory, labour lobbyists devote their attention to issues which are the subject of policy resolutions from the biennial conferences of the AFL-CIO (or their union) or of the Executive Council of the AFL-CIO (or their union). This can, if taken too seriously, convey an impression of labour lobbyists implementing policy which has welled up from the rank and file through the union structure. Such an impression would be seriously misleading, for American unions are no more successful than British (and arguably slightly less) in involving their membership in policy making. Indeed the commitment by labour lobbyists to certain issues, such as civil rights, might have been impossible to sustain if a more democratic or participatory structure had given the ordinary union member more influence over policy. Bok and Dunlop have reminded us that there is evidence which suggests that union officials are considerably more liberal than their members.[36] Moreover, it is at least as common for labour lobbyists to ask the Executive Council or Conference to adopt a policy resolution in order to strengthen their hand as it is for the Executive Council to give them a policy position to pursue. Thus in the campaign against the Carswell nomination the Executive Council adopted a resolution criticising his selection in order to demonstrate that the opposition to him rested on more than the whims of lobbyists. On other occasions, the AFL-CIO lobbyists work on an issue which neither the Executive Council nor the conference have considered. What, then, are the real sources of policy?

First, there are the labour lobbyists themselves. AFL-CIO lobbyists claim to have much discretion in deciding which topic to pursue, and how vigorously to pursue them.[37] However, they normally take the precaution of ensuring that Meany approves of their position. The close personal ties between the chief of the legislative section, Andrew Biemiller, and Meany also ensure that little is done without his approval. As Meany's influence over the Executive Council is enormous, a lobbyist who has obtained his approval can press ahead with guaranteed backing. Though this may act as a brake on the lobbyists, it neither limits their freedom completely, nor does it take from them the opportunity to set the agenda by selecting the issues on which the AFL-CIO might work. The discretion which the lobbyists enjoy is important for two reasons. First, labour lobbyists are commonly people of views very different from most Americans or, indeed, most American union officials. The influence of social democratic thinking has been surprisingly significant. Biemiller himself came to the AFL-CIO after working on a dissertation on the British labour movement and a brief spell in Congress, during which he managed to be labelled a socialist.[38] The lobbyists he recruited are of the same mould. The politically active unions, such as the UAW and AFSCME, also attract people of similar views who have decided that working as a labour union lobbyist is the best way to advance their views. Such people will use their discretion to become involved in as many liberal social issues as they are allowed.

This freedom and discretion affects their agenda in another way too. The labour lobbyists have implicit alliances with pressure groups of similar views, groups such as the NAACP, the National Farmers' Union or, to a lesser extent, Common Cause. Very frequently, lobbyists from these organisations will swop favours with the AFL-CIO. Labour lobbyists may have particularly good links to a congressman or senator from Pennsylvania while the National Farmers' Union has close ties to rural liberals, such as the Democrats from the Dakotas. AFL-CIO lobbyists may well help the NFU by urging urban congressmen to vote for farm subsidies; the NFU will encourage rural legislators to back repeal of 14(b) of Taft-Hartley. More commonly, both will work for general measures on which they are agreed. Congressmen, senators or administration lobbyists too may solicit the help of the labour lobbyists in securing votes. Such cooperation does not represent crude log-rolling; rather, it reflects the role of the AFL-CIO as a centre of a loose but steady coalition of liberal interest groups, each of which has specialised interests and concerns but which find cooperation is easy because they have common beliefs and attitudes. Indeed, lobbyists have moved between the AFL-CIO, Common Cause, the UAW and AFSCME without feeling that they had substantially changed the nature or direction of their work. There is little doubt that the AFL-CIO became involved in opposing the nomination of Carswell to the Supreme Court at the prompting of the ADA, the NAACP and other regular allies. The AFL-CIO or UAW lobbyists involved in the campaign expected no immediate pay-off in return; rather, they saw opposing Carswell as but one example of obligations which liberal pressure groups feel to help each other.

Finally, it is not unknown for an issue of general significance to be taken up by unions because of their industrial experience. As we have seen, National Health Insurance became one of labour's highest priorities only after the UAW had found that negotiations with the auto companies had almost broken down because the companies had put up strenuous resistance to meeting the cost of private health insurance for union members and their families. Similarly, the AFL-CIO's opposition to the nomination of Haynsworth to the Supreme Court arose in part because the unions knew that Haynsworth would be unsympathetic to labour unions in the numerous cases appealed to the Court from the National Labor Relations Board. The extensive system of labour law in the United States, the politics of which we shall discuss in a later chapter, ensures that labour unions cannot be indifferent to judicial politics; in practice, judges sympathetic to labour are liberal on other issues too.

There are, then, a variety of routes by which an issue can reach the top of the lobbyists' agenda. The political attitudes of the lobbyists, tactically and ideologically, prompt offers of help to other liberal groups; the industrial experience of labour unions themselves is the other principal way. The more important of these numerically are the personal preferences of the lobbyists as approved by the very top AFL-CIO officials or requests for help from friends and allies. Yet this suggests that the labour lobbyists' involvement, no matter how useful, is not the commitment of the broad masses of American labour. Lobbying is far from the experience of most union officials, let alone members. Indeed, occasionally the lobbyists go too far, and take up a position which the constituent unions will not support.

A clear example was the performance of the AFL-CIO over the Bolling Report. The Bolling Report constituted the most important attempt to reform the House of Representatives' Committee system since the 1940s. Bolling's Report was concerned not so much with shifting the balance of power within the House as with improving the efficiency and competence of the legislature so that it could recapture some of the ground lost to the executive branch. Far from being liberal or conservative, Bolling's Report was bipartisan. A congressman of considerable skill and experience, Bolling knew that his Committee's report would have little chance of success if important interests were offended by his proposals. As the Bolling Committee wished to divide the Education and Labor Committee in the interests of efficiency, Bolling realised the importance of securing the approval, or at least compliance, of the labour lobbyists. Bolling had good reason to believe that he had secured this. Apart from private assurances, Andrew Biemiller himself testified before the Bolling Committee, apparently accepting the proposals they had in mind.[39]

Within months of Biemiller's testimony to the Bolling Committee, the AFL-CIO had switched to vigorous opposition of the Bolling Report. The reasons why, apart from the importance of the issue, provide an interesting case study of the politics of labour lobbying. Bolling, himself a loyal friend of the labour lobbyists, had used his friendship to win Biemiller's support for his proposals. The labour lobbyists had themselves been divided about this. Some had argued from the start that splitting Education and Labor would either leave unions exposed to industrial relations legislation hostile to labour, or, if the friends of labour, as was probable, were reappointed to a new Labor committee, would make the new Education Committee more conservative. As the Education and Labor Committee has created much liberal legislation of general importance (such as the Economic Opportunity Act), the Bolling reforms, avowedly politically neutral, would weaken the liberals. At this stage, another congressman, with even better relations with organised labour, entered the picture. Representative Frank Thompson (Democrat, New Jersey) accepted the liberal case against Bolling just outlined. Moreover, Thompson can expect to become chairman of the Education and Labor Committee through the seniority system. Defeated amongst the Washington lobbyists by Biemiller's acceptance of the Bolling Report, Thompson appealed beyond them to the Executive of the AFL-CIO which happened to be in session. There, Thompson's appeal was not to the political predilections of its members but to the self-interest of the Maritime Unions. One of Bolling's other major proposals was to reform the Merchant Marine and Fisheries Committee, a committee which the maritime unions have cultivated extensively and expensively. Alerted by Thompson, the maritime unions insisted on a change of lobbying policy.[40] Thereby, they demonstrated that the discretion of the labour lobbyists, even at the very highest level, is not absolute.

LABOUR LOBBYISTS: CRITICISMS, PROSPECTS AND STRENGTH

The account of labour lobbyists presented here is one which many liberal academics will find surprisingly agreeable. Labour lobbyists have been presented as not only well organised and competent, but surprisingly wide ranging and liberal in the goals that they pursue. Yet many, including those close to the AFL-CIO, would take a less favourable view of its activities. There are two strands of criticism that should be distinguished.

First, there are those who believe that the AFL-CIO is insufficiently aggressive. They argue that one of the distinctive features of the AFL-CIO as a pressure group is that it has not only a distinguished group of lobbyists working for it but has an impressive electoral machine in the Committee on Political Education. Yet the AFL-CIO tends to follow a strategy in which it distinguishes the two aspects of its political work. Its lobbyists do not threaten electoral reprisals and, indeed, maintain a certain organisational distance from COPE. The political unions outside the AFL-CIO do not go in for such subtle distinctions, and neither do all of those within it. The United Auto Workers, the Machinists, AFSCME and even the ILGWU do not bother to distinguish lobbying from electoral action. Indeed the UAW emphasises the links between the two. To some degree, this sort of difference represents the legacy of the distinction between the AFL and CIO. The AFL, so far as it was involved in politics, followed a legislative or lobbying approach. The CIO was much more involved in electoral campaigning. There is also a contemporary difference over strategy. If, its critics argue, the AFL-CIO had been prepared to use its electoral muscle more, and less inclined to seek the best compromise available within Congress, then it would have been more successful over the long run. The point, it is argued, is not to manoeuvre within Congress but to change it. Even friendly congressmen have echoed the criticism. Abner Mikva told the *Congressional Quarterly* that the AFL-CIO made too many concessions on oil taxes in its campaign to get a general tax cut and reform through.[41]

Such complaints are hard to assess objectively. Many of those who stress them are men and women who are frustrated by the failure to build a fully fledged labour movement in the United States. One doubts that their dream can be fulfilled. On a more mundane level, other replies can be made to their criticisms. Thus Ken Young commented on Mikva's criticism, 'We may have misjudged it.'[42] Particularly in the current period of high turnover amongst congressmen and senators, labour lobbyists may be forgiven an occasional mistake. Mistakes apart, are Mikva and the other critics right? It is well to recall some of the points which we have encountered already. First, the conclusion of the preceding chapter was that though the electoral machinery of labour is impressive, it is not all powerful. COPE cannot rampage through the country bringing defeat to any senator or congressman it dislikes. Indeed, though an impressive organisation, its ability to deliver its members' votes, at least at the presidential level, is strictly limited. We must not jump from arguing correctly that labour is electorally significant to arguing that it is electorally all powerful. Labour lobbyists cannot realistically threaten all that many legislators. Certainly, few legislators from the South or South West would tremble at a threat from a union lobbyist. A Northern congressman would have more to fear, but he is not doomed by labour's curse either. The question arises whether labour lobbyists are supposed to give up the chance of immediate, if modest, gains until the composition of Congress has been changed by failing to cultivate legislators COPE might wish to replace. This raises a familiar question about the value of incremental gains and is one which prompts a debate which is not entirely scientific. It is, however, possible to make some comments.

The most important of these is that labour on its own has never been able to win. When the labour lobbyists have been isolated, they have always lost badly. This has been true even of Congresses in which the Democrats, even liberal Democrats, have a clear majority. When labour was isolated from the liberals during stages of the debate on Landrum-Griffin in 1959, it lost. When labour, breaking with its liberal allies, proposed restrictive trade laws in the 1970s, it lost equally badly. It is ironical that the same article in the *Congressional Quarterly* which gave currency to the view that AFL-CIO lobbyists were too soft also noted that when they tried to raise the level of public expenditure set by the Budget Committee (which liberals tended to support and wished to see firmly established), the AFL-CIO lobbyists lost in the Senate by a margin of 29–64. Labour lobbyists are entitled to conclude that while the gains from a greater recourse to electoral action are, to put it mildly, uncertain, the costs of breaking with existing friends are all too certain. Labour needs to be part of a coalition in Congress. As such, its power will not be absolute, but its influence will remain significant, subject to a proviso which will be noted below.

The second major strand of criticism of the labour lobbyists, and particularly those of the AFL-CIO, is that they are becoming more conservative or parochial. According to this view, though there is no doubt that labour made a notable and praiseworthy contribution to liberal legislation in the 1960s, it has relapsed into parochialism.

Some of the answers to this have been given elsewhere. The current preoccupation with the recession is both understandable and of benefit to many minority groups in America. The involvement of the AFL-CIO in causes such as civil rights (as shown by its opposition to Carswell) or support for National Health Insurance continues. Yet there are three areas in which the AFL-CIO's views are thought to be particularly significant – foreign affairs, trade policy and congressional reform.

There is no doubt, as we shall see later, that the AFL-CIO has been a vehement critic of detente and supporter of Soviet dissidents. Whether or not this should count as evidence of conservatism is uncertain. The

AFL-CIO has made little distinction between European authoritarian regimes of the extreme left or right which suppress liberties (including the right to form free trade unions). It is, of course, the case that most liberals in the United States have felt that the best approach to foreign affairs is to seek closer relations with the Soviet Union in the hope that a relaxation of tension (the official definition of detente) will aid Soviet dissidents more than would confrontation. The United Auto Workers and several unions within the AFL-CIO agree. Though complex theories may be constructed to explain why the American working class or unions are 'imperialist', a simpler explanation may suffice. As early as 1959, Irwin Ross, in a sympathetic account of Meany's career, noted that in issues of foreign policy, 'he seems to confuse principle with inflexibility'.[43] Barbash summarised the political position of labour in the 1950s as 'welfare state within the framework of a private enterprise system and anti-Communist internationalism'.[44] Meany has not acquired greater flexibility as he has aged. His foreign policy attitudes remain today as they were twenty years ago. At that time Meany would have been in the mainstream of liberal thinking on foreign policy. Since then, liberals have changed their attitudes, while Meany has not. In this, as in so much else, the question remains whether the problem to be explained is the shift in attitude by liberals or the stability of attitudes amongst the aged leadership of the AFL-CIO. Even their critics should admit, however, that the AFL-CIO's foreign policy position is more complex than a simple labelling as 'conservative'. The well publicised hostility of the AFL-CIO to detente needs matching by reference to the AFL-CIO's lobbying against the lifting of sanctions against Rhodesia in order to allow the United States to buy chrome.[45]

Yet neither should we imagine that the AFL-CIO has devoted much of its lobbying effort to broad principles of foreign policy. In fact, the labour lobbyists have been relatively inactive on foreign policy, a fact which reflects their unwillingness to undermine good relations with liberals. As the 1960s drew to a close, it became harder and harder to find liberal legislators who favoured continuing the Vietnam War. Even the AFL-CIO's favourites, such as Frank Thompson, went 'doveish'. Meany had sufficient calibre to recognise that stable friendships should not be ended on such issues. Indeed, congressmen generally well disposed to the AFL-CIO, but in disagreement with its foreign policy, reported no pressure at all on the subject. It is symptomatic that when George Meany did in fact make an appearance before the Senate Foreign Relations Committee to criticise detente, his bitterest exchange was with Senator Jacob Javits (Republican, New York). In the very next election (1974) Javits was one of the very few Republicans to be endorsed by the AFL-CIO.[46]

Though labour lobbyists have been comparatively inactive on foreign policy issues, they have not been inactive on foreign trade. In the early 1960s, the AFL-CIO won praise from liberal economists for its support for the Trade Expansion Act which gave the President authority to negotiate to cut tariffs. In exchange, the unions were given a clause in the Act providing help to those who lost their jobs in consequence. By 1973, however, the AFL-CIO had swung round to protectionism and had a bill introduced by Senator Hartke and Representative Burke, which would have limited foreign countries' exports to their level in 1965–9. Labour was no more monolithic on foreign trade than on foreign policy. Though I. W. Abel (President of the Steelworkers and of the AFL-CIO's Industrial Union Department) appeared to support the bill,[47] Leonard Woodcock, President of the UAW, spoke against. His testimony, however, indicated the pressure which even that liberal union felt on the issue.

> The UAW still supports liberal international trade policies. We are still able to convince delegates elected by the rank and file of the wisdom of that course, but trade liberalisation must be accompanied by measures that will protect workers and their families against victimisation if we are to continue in that posture.[48]

Without indulging in special pleading on behalf of the AFL-CIO, it is fair to note that advocacy of import controls and a 'siege economy' is regarded in some countries such as Britain as a left wing cause. The foreign trade issue is another which provides unconvincing evidence that the AFL-CIO has shifted to the right. It does, however, suggest that economic hardship increases the sectional concerns and lobbying activity of unions. Faced with the worst recession since the 1930s the AFL-CIO lobbyists have attached a much higher priority to issues which contribute to saving jobs in the short term. As argued above, the idea that hard times radicalise unions dies hard. Yet the American experience is surely that hard times do serve to narrow labour's political concerns.

The final issue advanced to prove that the AFL-CIO lobbyists have become more conservative in their attitude to congressional reform. The arguments on this have been advanced already in our discussion of the Bolling Committee's Report. Suffice to say that the crucial difference is between the favourable attitude of the AFL-CIO to reforms which shift the balance of power in favour of liberals, and its indifference to reforms which merely improve the efficiency of Congress. The AFL-CIO's lobbyists have not been active on the 'clean government' issues of the 1970s unless, like limitations on campaign contributions or postal voter registration, it has seen a pay-off in terms of diminishing the power of its enemies. If there has been any conflict between labour's political advantage and congressional reform, the labour lobbyists ultimately (as with the Bolling Report) have safeguarded the former to the detriment of the latter. Calculated purely in terms of short term advantage, the AFL-CIO lobbyists were right to conclude that splitting Education and Labor would have weakened their position. Whether the revival of congressional power which such reforms were designed to achieve is to labour's advantage or not is imponderable.

More important than the desirability or otherwise of the AFL-CIO's attitude to congressional reform is the gap which has opened between liberal thinking and the AFL-CIO. In the 1950s and 1960s, the liberal programme was concerned with policy outputs. Issues such as civil rights, full employment, Medicare and generally expanding and improving America's embryonic welfare state provided a platform which could unite liberals and the unions; their objectives were more or less identical. Now they are not. The contemporary liberal has different concerns. The 1960s and 1970s have given liberals good cause to be interested in procedural reforms. Both Vietnam and Watergate have been associated with, if not explained by, the decline in the power of Congress, the importance of money in American elections and the need for 'open' government. In short, liberalism in the 1970s in America has been considerably concerned with, for obvious reasons, the application of the principles of consumerism to politics. Labour lobbyists tend to look at such issues, see the absence of any clear social class content, and lose interest. Indeed, though working with the consumer movement in legislation affecting the private sector, labour lobbyists have been indifferent to the sorts of issue that concern Common Cause; some go futher and view such organisations as a diversion from major political objectives. Whereas the Common Cause lobbyists feel that the AFL-CIO stopped developing in the 1960s politically, the AFL-CIO lobbyists view Common Cause (not without justification) as a predominantly middle class pressure group which takes no interest in social reform, anti-poverty legislation or the day to day problems of working Americans. On a personal level, Biemiller lacks the *rapport* with the new liberals he has with 'old' liberals such as Frank Thompson.[49]

The most serious problem the labour lobbyists face is that recent liberal recruits to Congress are more like Common Cause and less like themselves. The *Congressional Quarterly* report on the labour lobbyists probably was correct in its estimate that the number of senators who instinctively responded to the spending proposals favoured by the AFL-CIO had fallen from between 38 and 42 to less than 30. The trend reflects the fact that, along with the development of interest in procedural reforms, liberals have lost faith in the orthodox (and not so orthodox) solutions to social problems which, it is claimed, 'failed' in the Great Society. Not all the liberal senators, if any, are as sceptical as, say, Governor Brown of California in their attitude to the capacity of government to manage social change or reform. Yet there is an inevitable lack of imagination at the highest levels of the AFL-CIO caused by the age of its leaders which is open to criticism. The fashionable scepticism amongst liberals about important issues which the labour lobbyists have fought to achieve, but have not yet accomplished, is not entirely to the liberals' credit either. As the liberals are still concerned with social issues, they would do well to bear in mind the legislative priorities which Meany presented to Johnson immediately after the assassination of President Kennedy. These were the civil rights bill, a tax cut and measures to ameliorate unemployment, and Medicare. Reuther added 'education' to the list.[50] This mixture of self-interest and altruism at the highest levels of the AFL-CIO in the past provided the basis for a fruitful partnership between liberals and labour. It could do so again in the future. In the meantime, the contribution of the labour lobbyists to general causes should not be forgotten.

THE EFFECTIVENESS OF THE LABOUR LOBBYISTS

At this point, it is necessary to add a cautious conclusion by returning to the beginning and placing labour in the context of our general knowledge of lobbying. No one seriously suggests anymore that any lobbyist can dominate a congressman totally. Senators are equally unlikely to be cowed. The work of the lobbyist is to argue, cajole, persuade and organise. These the labour lobbyists, as we have seen, do unusually well. Yet their impact, like that of all lobbyists, is limited. Labour lobbyists have to work with the legislators they have to hand, and in that sense the efforts made through COPE and individual unions to influence the composition of Congress are more important in the long term than the lobbyists' manoeuvres with legislators.

A FLAGGING HIERARCHY?

Though the general competence of the AFL-CIO's lobbyists remains unquestioned, the start of the 95th Congress and the advent of the Carter Administration brought fresh questioning of the ability of the trio who make crucial tactical political decisions for the AFL-CIO, namely Meany, the chief lobbyist, Andy Biemiller, and the head of COPE, Al Barkan. By 1977, Barkan, who was 68, was the youngest of the trio. That relations with the new President worsened after the election could be explained by the dubious commitment of the new President to such traditionally liberal Democratic goals endorsed by labour as National Health Insurance or reflation. However, the leadership of the AFL-CIO was also responsible for the worsening of relations by intransigently pressing certain demands that the President was naturally unwilling to meet (such as renominating President Ford's one time Secretary of Labor, John Dunlop, to that office). If unions had reason to be suspicious of a President who received memoranda from his staff urging him to concentrate on purely symbolic acts during the first part of his Presidency, the President was apparently given good reason to believe that the union leaders were dogmatic and even just rude.

Similar problems arose in dealing with Congress. Congress had, of course, a large Democratic majority; the Democratic successes of 1974 when Watergate and depression had hit the Republicans badly were not reversed in 1976. The Congress was also said to be liberal. However, commentators suspected that this liberalism was not in the tradition of the New Deal and Hubert Humphrey but like Carter, and Governors Brown of California and Dukakis of Massachusetts, it represented suspicions of 'big government' and 'special interests', including labour. It was astonishing, therefore, that the leadership of the AFL-CIO confronted this Congress as its first test of its attitude to labour with a piece of 'special interest' legislation, the 'situs' picketing bill designed to increase power of the construction unions. Though a 'situs' picketing bill had been passed in the previous Congress, it had done so only with the (temporary) support of President Ford and Secretary of Labor, John Dunlop. (Ford later vetoed the bill.) Carter announced that he would sign the bill, but would not campaign for it in Congress. Though Carter's Secretary of Labor, F. Ray Marshall, did lend the bill his support, the absence of full backing from the Administration, coupled with the now unrestrained hostility of the Republicans, more or less guaranteed the bill's defeat. In spite of this, however, the AFL-CIO pressed freshmen congressmen to complicate their relations with their districts (which were often not blue collar areas) by voting for the bill. Some refused; those who obliged felt that they had fulfilled their post-election obligations to labour by voting for an unpopular (and doomed) measure.

Labour has traditionally enjoyed little success and exhibited little skill in working for changes in the labour laws. Yet by any criteria, the high priority placed on the common 'situs' picketing bill was unwise. If the bill had succeeded, it would have benefited only construction unions. Its failure blocked attempts to repeal Section 14(b) of Taft-Hartley which would have helped every union recruit more members. Not only can one argue that it would have been in the best traditions of the AFL-CIO to put a more general issue first on its list of priorities rather than a pure labour bill, but it is also likely that such a strategy, by cementing relations with liberal legislators, would have improved the chances of passing a common situs picketing bill, or repeal of Section 14(b) of Taft-Hartley. The most that the AFL-CIO will obtain from the present Congress is an act to reduce the opportunities for employers to delay cases which are before the National Labor Relations Board.

From the perspective of the unions, an optimistic interpretation of this incident is that President Meany, who came from and received much support from the construction unions, wished to make their gratification his prime objective before retiring. A more pessimistic view is that no such retirement or beneficence was intended; the AFL-CIO's gerentocracy was merely losing its touch. Time will tell.

5 Politics and the Union Member

So far, this study has been concerned with the political behaviour of unions as organisations. Our focus has been on the purposes, methods and efficiency of their intervening in elections or in lobbying legislators. The degree to which unions are successful in such work obviously depends in part on the extent to which they have the support of their members. If, as is so frequently the case in Britain, the political attitudes of the union hierarchies are at variance with those of the bulk of the membership, the political impact of the unions will be reduced. If, in contrast, unions are pressing for policies which their members endorse, their effectiveness will be greater.

The political efforts of organised labour in the United States have been directed, to a surprising degree, to the furthering of general liberal domestic policy. Causes such as civil rights legislation, anti-poverty programmes and the creation of a national health service have received significant help from the unions. In spite of this, however, a tendency has emerged to assume that union members themselves are intolerant, bigoted and conservative. Bok and Dunlop have produced evidence to suggest that liberalism on civil rights is much more common in the higher reaches of unions than amongst the rank and file.[1] On the right, writers such as Kevin Phillips[2] have argued that the white working class is a potential recruit for the emerging Republican majority, a view which gained credence after the capture by President Nixon of a majority of votes from blue collar workers in the 1972 elections. The liberal intelligentsia, traditionally allied with the working class in the Democratic Party, has shown signs of agreeing with Phillips. It became commonplace to point to the attacks by 'hardhats' (i.e construction workers) on predominantly middle class protestors against the American 'incursion' into Laos and Cambodia in 1970 as an illustration of the aggressive or 'hawkish' views of the American worker on foreign policy. It was assumed that the white worker, himself newly arrived in the suburbs from the inner city, would fear the arrival of black families and resent government programmes to help blacks. In short, the white working class was assumed to be not only 'hawkish' in attitudes on foreign policy but also hostile to civil rights legislation. Moreover, it was argued by liberals, the crucial issues in American politics were decreasingly concerned with economic or social issues (such as had been the case during the New Deal): the crucial issues were increasingly about 'life styles' or individual behaviour, the use of drugs being an example of such a question. On such questions the ill-educated, often Catholic, worker could be assumed to be a fierce defender of 'decency'. The working class, strongly attached to the American system within which it hoped to make progress, was· assumed too to be hostile to student demonstrations and other groups exercising their civil liberties. Finally, perhaps because they were thought to be bearing the brunt of increased crime, the white working class were thought to be hostile to any attempts by liberals to reduce penalties or otherwise soften the criminal law. A number of comic, fictional characters, such as Archie Bunker were created in the media to voice the thoughts of the overweight, stupid, drunken and, it appeared, conservative, white worker. Liberal Democrats, argued the men who advised McGovern,[3] should rely on coalitions of the young, the poor and women, not on workers. Even the white middle class, through adroit use of issues such as 'the environment' would provide a better prospect for the future than the working class. Perhaps fortunately (from the perspective of such liberals) it has been argued that the blue collar worker is a disappearing creature. Technological change has produced a situation in which there are more white than blue collar workers in the USA.[4]

All of the assertions above about the political attitudes of the white workers have been challenged by a series of committed, but persuasive studies.

The message of these studies is clear. The United States is not becoming a 'middle class' country. The highly publicised shift from blue to white collar occupations is accounted for by a growth in service occupations, such as being a shop assistant, which are not usually what is imagined to be middle class occupations (particularly when the person concerned is married to a blue collar worker). Similarly, the usual description of clerical staff as being not merely clerical white collar but also 'middle class' is questionable. Levison,[5] leaning on the excellent work in this field by Richard Hamilton,[6] argues that the proportion of male workers who are in working class occupations is not 37.5 per cent but 57.5 per cent. Levison argues that even 55.3 per cent of *white* males are in blue collar jobs. Nor is the trend from 'working class' to 'middle class' posts rapid; between 1950 and 1969, Levison claims, the proportion in working class occupations fell by merely 5 per cent of the total. Such growth as there has been in middle class posts has been in the technical or educational spheres in response to political, not commercial decisions.

Trends in the occupational distribution of the working class have caused probably less concern than its political attitudes. Debate has been joined hotly on the liberalism or conservatism of American workers. Most writers, including Hamilton, have found that American workers are more liberal on economic issues than are the middle classes; that is to say, American workers are more likely to favour federal action to overcome social or economic disadvantage than are their middle class

TABLE 5.1: *Liberal Attitudes on Domestic Issues amongst Manual and Non-Manual Workers*

	Non-South, *Non Manuals*			
Issue	*Income to $10,000*		*Income over $10,000*	
	Self-employed, retired, etc.	*Salaried*	*Self-employed, retired, etc.*	*Salaried*
Percentage of those with opinions on the questions asked giving liberal responses				
Medical care	52	57	40	49
Living standards	26	36	26	24
School aid	35	36	36	40
Government too powerful	53	58	41	45

	Non-South, *Manuals*	
Issue	*Income up to $7,500*	*Over $7,500*
Percentage of those with opinions on the questions asked giving liberal responses		
Medical care	86 (70)	70 (51)
Living standards	61 (38)	36 (45)
School aid	51 (39)	44 (34)
Government too powerful	75 (68)	70 (56)

NB Figures in brackets are for white Protestant workers.
Source: Compiled from Richard Hamilton, *Class and Politics in the United States*, p. 399–420.

counterparts. Action by the federal government to put health care within the reach of all is a common example. Hamilton extends the analysis by comparing attitudes on four economic questions amongst white male workers outside the South. The liberal position on the issues he examined was to favour provision of medical insurance by the federal government, expect the federal government to accept responsibility for living standards, approve of federal aid to schools and to reject the claim that the federal government was too powerful. Using 1964 data, Hamilton found the distribution of opinion shown in Table 5.1.

Rather surprisingly, the findings which Hamilton reports, and which are accepted as more or less standard, are somewhat contradicted by more recent work by Howard Reiter.[7] Focussing on 'lower middle income members of the white race making an annual income from $4,000 to $8,000 in 1968', Reiter argued that 'lower middle class blue collar whites do not differ from the rest of the population' or else are a bit more '*conservative* on most important questions relevant to New Deal issues'. Only in their attitude to unions were the members of his target group more liberal (i.e. favourable).

Reiter, however, expected this surprising finding to be invalidated as economic recession worsened. His major argument was that white workers were *not* unusually conservative on non-economic questions. His general conclusion was 'that while white Americans tend to be less than ardent civil rights advocates and Americans in general strongly support authority figures and oppose protesters, lower middle income blue collar whites are somewhat more conservative than other groups. . . . *But it is also* clear that on these issues blue collar America *is not far from the mainstream*' (emphasis added).[8]

The difference between Hamilton and Reiter is almost certainly explained by Hamilton's exclusion of the South. This can be defended on the grounds that the South is different, that in the South the categories used pull in many who are, or have been, farmworkers, not part of the industrial working class, and by reminding ourselves that the argument is supposedly about the urban working class outside the South anyway. Only in the case of attitudes towards civil disobedience and liberties are Hamilton and Levison forced to concede that the blue collar worker is more conservative. In particular, American workers displayed a strong dislike for student protests.

In contrast, Levison and Hamilton argue that blue collar workers are very slightly *more* disposed to favour civil rights legislation. Thus Hamilton arrived at the following picture of non-Southern opinion in 1968:

TABLE 5.2: *Civil Rights Attitudes of Non South Whites by Class, 1968 (married white respondents, employed)*
Percentage in favour (of those with opinions on the questions asked)

Issue	Operative, Service Industries Labourers	Skilled	Lower Middle	Upper Middle
Government should see that Negroes get fair treatment in jobs	49	44	43	45
Government should see that Negroes can go to any hotel or restaurant	67	62	64	65
Government should see to it that white and Negro children go to the same schools	55	40	48	47
Negroes have a right to live wherever they can afford to	82	88	85	82

Source: Richard Hamilton, 'Black Demands, White Reactions and Liberal Alarms', in Levitan (ed.) *op. cit.*, p. 135.

TABLE 5.3: *Attitudes towards Student Protests*

	Blue collar	White collar
High hostility to student demonstrations (1970)	50	30
Student protests and demonstrations unjustified (1970)	62	53
Student protest is violence (only union members surveyed on this)	43	–
Draftcard burning is violence	63	NA
Police beating students is violence (only union members surveyed on this)	45	NA

Source: Levitan, *op. cit.*, p. 161.

Such findings should be interpreted as showing a dislike of violence, not of fondness for involvement in the Vietnam War. Indeed, for a variety of reasons, including a tendency to favour extreme solutions, a slightly higher proportion of workers favoured quick withdrawal from Vietnam than did the middle classes.

TABLE 5.4: *Percentage of Northern Whites in Favour of Immediate Withdrawal from Vietnam (or within 18 months) 1970*

Working class	48.9 %
Middle class	40.9 %

Source: Levison, *op. cit.*

It is worth stressing that so far our focus has been mainly on the attitudes of working class Americans in general, not of union members alone. For a variety of reasons, union members can be expected to be more liberal than American workers in general. Unions, after all, have most of their strength outside the conservative South and in more liberal areas such as the North East. Moreover, American voting returns show a steady tendency for American union members to vote Democratic more heavily than workers in general. We shall turn now to an examination of the political allegiance of members of families where at least one member belongs to a union. In order to minimise the impact of factors other than policies or allegiance which affect elections, (voters' assessment of the competence of a candidate may be of tremendous importance in influencing presidential elections) our focus shall be on mid-term elections.

TABLE 5.5: *Party Identification, 1970*[9]

	Union Families	National Sample
Strong Democrat	25.4 } 53.8	19.8 } 43.5
Not very strong Democrat	28.4	23.7
Independent closer to Democrat	10.7	10.4
Independent closer to neither	14.7	12.9
Independent closer to Republican	5.7	7.8
Not very strong Republican	10.2 } 14.2	15.3 } 24.5
Strong Republican	4.0	9.2
Other minor party, refused to say	0.5	0.2
Apolitical	0.5	0.7

Union families, as we would expect, are noticeably more Democratic in their party identification than the nation as a whole. Similarly, the proportion of union members who identify with the Republican Party is lower. However, it is worth noting that these tendencies are not massive; the difference with the national sample in the proportion of union families identifying with the Democrats is only 10.3. It is interesting to see how these figures translated into votes in the 1970 mid-term elections. It is worth remembering that the 1970 elections overall were ones in which the Democrats and liberals in Congress more or less held their ground, but came under strong pressure from the Nixon Administration and in particular the strident Vice President, Spiro Agnew, who made a major effort to defeat liberals from both parties.

TABLE 5.6:   *Voting for senators – 1970*[10]
             (percentage distribution)

	Union Families	National Sample
Democratic	67.8	58.1
Republican	27.3	36.5
New York Conservative	2.7	3.2
Other	2.2	2.2

Once again, the tendency for union families to prefer Democrats to Republicans is strong. Unfortunately, as the Democrats are now so successful, they dominate Congress by a massive margin, and so the difference between union families and the national sample is steady, but not strong.

TABLE 5.7:   *Votes for House of Representatives – 1970*[11]
             (percentage distribution)

	Union Families	National Sample
Democratic	65.9	54.0
Republican	32.4	45.1
Minor party	1.7	0.9

The results are so similar to those for the Senate as to need little comment. Union families compared with the national sample showed a steady but not massive tendency to favour Democrats and dislike Republicans. The same was true in gubernatorial elections.

Finally, it is interesting to compare the willingness of union families to accept the idea that there are social classes with that of the national sample.

TABLE 5.8:   *Voting in the Gubernatorial Elections – 1970*[12]
              (Percentage distribution)

	Union Families	National Sample
Democratic	65.4	49.0
Republican	34.0	49.5
Minor party	0.6	1.5

TABLE 5.9:   *Social attitudes in comparison to that of the national sample*[13]

	Union Families	National Sample
	(% answering 'yes')	
Think of self as belonging to working or middle class	67.8	63.6
Do not think of belonging to working or middle class	31.9	35.9
Refuse to accept idea of classes	0.3	0.1
Other	–	0.3
Don't know	–	–
Not available	–	–

Union families clearly are a little more ready to see America in society in terms of classes than the national sample; however, the difference again is small.

CONCLUSIONS

The argument about the liberalism or conservatism of the American working class is inevitably sharp. The motives of the protagonists are not only to advance social science but also to demonstrate the viability of a liberal strategy relying on working class support, on the one hand, and the need to look for a constituency amongst young professionals, on the other.

The evidence seems to support neither side satisfactorily. It is certainly the case that the allegations that the American worker is racist and reactionary seem ill-founded. American workers are very slightly more liberal on race, and only on certain civil liberties questions (particularly those generated by student demonstrations) are workers noticeably more right wing than the rest of the population. Indeed, the striking, though little-emphasised, implication of most of the surveys of working class attitudes is that the American worker is very little different from the population as a whole. On race, foreign policy and even, prior to recent recessions, on economic issues, the division of opinion amongst American workers is very similar to that amongst the population as a whole. If the myth of a reactionary American working class should be laid to rest, so should that of the working class as a hidden reservoir of support for radical change.

Our concern is not to join the controversy about the liberalism or conservatism of the American working class. It is rather to draw attention to the implications for the political power of unions. If American workers had appeared particularly conservative, then the political action programme of the AFL-CIO and unions would have seemed a paper tiger with little real support. In fact, though American workers are not zealous radicals they are unlikely to be hostile to the reformist programme favoured by the AFL-CIO and politically active unions. Similarly, American workers, like their unions, are inclined to favour the Democrats by a margin which is steadily, if unspectacularly, greater than that for the population as a whole. The American working class, in brief, is not a social group set apart from the rest of society by strongly held political beliefs; for better or worse, American union families are in the mainstream of popular opinion.

Most of the trade union movement in the United States has been unambiguously liberal on the major issues of domestic policy. Survey evidence suggests little in the political attitudes of the American working class to explain this. If the American worker is not recognisably more liberal than the rest of the country on many issues, the liberal position of the unions must reflect the views more of their officers and officials. On the other hand, the absence of a conservative majority amongst American workers makes it unlikely that union members would react against the policies and views of their leaders. To that extent, union leaders are given freedom of action if not enthusiastic support in their political activities.

6 The Governing of Labour

Both unions and employers in the United States have to contend with a vast array of federal law governing industrial relations. Neither employers nor unions have found this consistently to their advantage. The earliest National Labor Relations Acts in the 1930s were quite clearly designed to help unions. Indeed, had it not been for the Wagner Act which prohibited as 'unfair labor practices' such common tactics as the use of company spies, victimisation, threats of plant closures and promises of pay increases for employees if a union were rejected, it is questionable whether the CIO would have been able to organise some of the industries it did. The National Labor Relations Board (NLRB), which the Act created, made it possible for the first time for workers to choose freely in secret ballots whether or not to join a union. Later amendments to the National Labor Relations Act were, in contrast, clearly designed to weaken the unions. The Taft-Hartley Act of 1947, passed by a Republican Congress over the veto of President Truman, for the first time extended the concept of an unfair labour practice to the unions. The most important features of the Act were the prohibition of secondary boycotts (in which workers not directly affected by strikes or boycotts aided fellow workers involved in a dispute with someone other than their employer by refusing to handle his products), the '80-day cooling-off period' for which the President could order the suspension of a strike, restrictions on picketing and unionising supervisory staff, and Section 14(b) which allowed states to adopt legislation prohibiting the closed shop. The Landrum-Griffin Act of 1959 also slightly weakened the position of unions.

No simple summary of federal labour law is possible. After all, the labour laws generate thousands of cases each year, enough to demand the existence of a separate system of labour law courts and a body of lawyers and law firms specialising in the subject. It is possible, and indeed desirable, however, to distinguish the different objectives of federal labour law, particularly as these objectives are deliberately confused for political ends. In the first place, the law seeks to set the balance of power between employer and employee. This covers issues such as what constitutes unfair dismissal. It also, and more importantly for our purposes, covers the regulation of the balance of power between employers and unions, by means such as prohibiting the closed shop or secondary boycott. An entirely separate goal is that of preventing malpractice within the affairs of unions. Such provisions of the law provide for honest and fair elections, prescribe penalties for the many forms of corruption which have been practised by union officials and prohibit recently convicted criminals from holding union office. Finally, through use of the cooling-off period and the work of federal arbitrators, the federal laws aim at providing some insulation for the general public from disputes to which they are not a party.

It is a truism of particular importance in the United States that the politics of implementation is as important as the politics of legislating. It is very common for a law to be passed (such as the Economic Opportunity Act) but few resources to be put into the programme it creates. Similarly, the agencies charged with administering an act may choose or be compelled by Congress or the President to put much more emphasis on one part of the act than on another. Thus the power of unions in America and the integrity of their internal political process depends not just on the letter of the law but on its enforcement. Many, however, question the impartiality of the law's enforcement. The president of the AFL-CIO, George Meany, has argued recently that the implementation of federal labour law regulating the balance between employers and unions consistently favours the former.[1] However, it is more widely believed in the United States that all the agencies charged with administering the labour laws, the Department of Labor and its agencies, along with the National Labor Relations Board, are in the pocket of the unions. This chapter is concerned to examine the politics of the way in which federal labour law is actually implemented.

THE DEPARTMENT OF LABOR AND ITS SECRETARY

There is a general belief in the United States that all departments and their secretaries have to adapt themselves to the wishes of the interests which they serve, irrespective of the wishes of the President. The explanation for this is said to lie in the supposed fact that the interest groups with which a department deals dominate the congressmen and senators who sit on the congressional committees from which the department has to obtain legislation and appropriations.[2] Irrespective of the wishes of the President, a Department and its Secretary have to accommodate themselves to the wishes of these interest groups and committees. Indeed, in order to forestall trouble, a President might well appoint a Secretary from the ranks of a department's customers or, as they are usually termed, 'clientele'. This tendency for Departments to be dominated by their clientele is usually thought to be particularly strong in the case of the Departments of Agriculture, Commerce and Labor, partly because they were all formed to provide services to farmers, businessmen and workers, respectively.

Partly because of this belief, the Department of Labor has a weak position. It is a small department, being only one third the size of the next smallest department. Many of the developments in labour legislation, particularly those affecting the relative power of employers and unions, have been entrusted to the autonomous NLRB. The Department, it is true, was entrusted with enforcing laws on unions designed to prevent corruption, but this task as we shall see has complicated its relations with the unions. Whereas the Department was once an important institution in the implementation of social policy in the United States, most developments in that field have since been entrusted to new agencies. Under the War on Poverty, for example, even manpower training schemes went first to the Office of Economic Opportunity and then to the Department of Health, Education and Welfare. The Department of Labor has been left without any clear mission, frequently sharing policy areas with other departments. Only in the area of labour conciliation does the Department have the field to itself. In other areas it is expected to spell out the implications of a policy on the labour market and workers. While unions have, in the course of this century, become one of the most powerful social institutions in the United States, the Department of Labor has languished.

How justified are the allegations that the Department is dominated by the unions? It is true that the Department's officials are concerned primarily with the well-being of workers just as in Britain officials at the Ministries of Agriculture, Education and Industry are concerned primarily with the well-being of, respectively, agriculture, education and industry. Thus, when officials of the Labor Department and its Secretary attend meetings concerned with trade agreements, they are concerned naturally to spell out the implications of a trade deal on employment. This in itself is scarcely proof of capture by the Department's clientele, particularly as the Department's conception of what serves the interest of American workers will change. Thus, during the Ford Administration, although nearly all unions were critical of moves to liberalise trade because they believed that there would be an increase in imports and consequently an increase in unemployment, Republican officials within the Department believed that freer trade would increase exports and benefit workers overall.[3] Or, to take a different example, Democratic Secretaries of Labor and unions, on the one hand, tend to differ from Republican Secretaries, on the other, on the desirable level of the minimum wage. Democrats and unions believe in a higher minimum wage to help the non-unionised; Republicans fear that a higher minimum wage will discourage employers from filling posts which are low paid but also unproductive, so that unemployment will increase. Thus, even if the Labor Department dedicates itself to the interests of American workers, the practical definition of what constitutes that interest varies, and is often not in line with the interpretation favoured by the unions.

Though it is undeniably the case that the unions have considerable influence over both the House Education and Labor Committee's Democrats and the Democrats and some Republicans on the Senate Labor and Public Welfare Committee, as the previous paragraph suggests, this has not always been translated into dominance over the Department's Secretary, as the clientele theory would suggest. The reasons for this are varied. In the first place, the Secretary is not as central to unions' political strategy as the clientele theory supposes. The unions are too strong and the Department too weak for it to be otherwise. As George Meany once put it, 'I don't pay too much attention to the Secretary . . . if you have a problem with the building, you don't discuss it with the janitor.'[4] From the President's perspective, the political costs of appointing someone from the unions to head a Department which is in some measure their policeman, would be too high. This is primarily the reason why, as Domhoff notes, Secretaries of Labor rarely come from the unions.[5] Truman, Kennedy and Johnson chose lawyers like Willard Wirtz and Arthur Goldberg. Roosevelt appointed a reform minded member of the Boston upper class, Frances Perkins. Carter, like Kennedy, turned down all the nominations put forward by the AFL-CIO and chose an academic, F. Ray Marshall. It is true that Eisenhower appointed a Labor Secretary, Martin Durkin, who was President of the Plumbers' Union, and Nixon at one time had a Labor Secretary, Peter Brennan, from the New York Construction Workers, but neither experiment was long-lived or happy in its results. Eisenhower reverted to type after Durkin resigned and appointed James P. Mitchell, Vice President of Bloomingdales, the New York department store, Labor Secretary, while Ford reverted to an academic (John Dunlop) and a career civil servant, William Usery. Another reason for avoiding appointments from the ranks of the unions is that the splits and tensions within the labour movement make the selection of a Secretary from one camp or other too risky. Truman, Kennedy and Johnson could balance low level political appointments between craft and industrial unions. Such a strategy could not be followed for the Secretaryship or Under-Secretaryship. Indeed, at the lower level, Eisenhower had so much trouble that he decided it was not worth the effort. Mann and Doig report that

> the impasse over one union prospect resulted in mutual agreement that there would be no union representation in the high ranks of the Labor Department. As a result, from 1954, Eisenhower appointees in the Department of Labor were men with professional or business backgrounds.[6]

The major reason why the clientele theory of American politics presents a misleading picture of the Secretary of Labor is that it overlooks the importance of ideological attitudes to unions. One of the defining features of modern Republicanism has been hostility to unions, a point to which we shall return. This hostility has made it impossible for a Secretary of Labor to sustain a pro-union policy during a Republican administration. The proof of this came during the presidencies of Nixon and Ford.

By the end of 1972, forces much more important than clientelism were encouraging Republicans to look with renewed interest at the unions. Prior to the 1972 elections, there had been much discussion of how the 'social issue'[7] might split blue collar workers from the predominantly liberal Democratic Party. It was argued that blue collar workers would be concerned about crime, race and militant opposition to the Vietnam War so that they would switch to conservative Republicans. The refusal by the AFL-CIO to endorse Senator McGovern for the Presidency and the results in the Presidential election which showed that majorities of both blue collar workers and union families had voted for Nixon appeared to indicate that important parts of the working class and labour movement might be recruited for the 'emerging Republican majority'. Nixon was sufficiently impressed to make Brennan Secretary of Labor and initiate wide ranging, confidential talks with the leadership of the AFL-CIO. In short, there appeared to be widespread recognition that the future of the Republican Party might be advanced best by befriending the unions in general and the right wing unions in particular. Pre-eminent amongst the right wing unions, if only because of their influence within the AFL-CIO, were the construction unions.

The construction unions are renowned for the narrowness of their political goals. While the refusal by Presidents Nixon and Ford to spend their way out of the recession which gripped the western world in the 1970s more or less guaranteed the opposition of the bulk of the unions to Ford's election, the antagonism of the construction unions was less certain. Measures to help the construction industry and the construction unions in particular might have produced a repeat of the situation in 1972 when they pressed hard for the AFL-CIO to stay out of the Presidential campaign. The chief legislative objective of the construction unions had long been a measure known as common situs picketing, allowing the unions to picket a whole site and not just a subcontractor on it. Ford's Secretary of Labor, John Dunlop, was keen to tidy up the laws affecting labour relations within the construction industry, a subject on which he was an expert. The time was opportune to make a gesture. With Ford's permission, Dunlop conceded common 'situs' picketing and, indeed, Republicans in Congress were pressed with some success to support the bill. Ford then vetoed the bill without warning. The reason for this apparently inexplicable step was that Ford had become increasingly concerned about the threat Ronald Reagan posed to his struggle to win the Republican nomination. Ford decided that whatever the potential benefits in the November election, he could not afford to be labelled 'pro-union' by Reagan, whose appeal was to conservative Republicans, in the primaries. In brief, party considerations rooted in Republican antagonism to unions precluded a pro-union policy, even though electoral strategy reinforced clientele pressures. Dunlop felt obliged to resign and was replaced by a colourless official from the Labor Department whose political ventures were confined to paying extravagant compliments to a national convention of the thoroughly corrupt (but conservative) Teamsters union. For their part, the construction unions made an unusual commitment to the Democratic nominee, Carter.

Presidents from both parties have found picking Secretaries from the nominations submitted by unions unprofitable. Divisions amongst the unions have made the risk of offending more unions than are pleased too high. Moreover, Democrats have been afraid of seeming too closely linked to the unions. Republicans have occasionally taken the risk but have neither liked the results nor has their party been prepared to make the necessary concessions.

As Labor Secretaries are not the nominees of unions, let alone their officials, it is not surprising that they resent the belief that they are, particularly as the effect on their Department's standing has been sharp. When Johnson's Labor Secretary, Willard Wirtz, was asked if, as Johnson planned, it was possible to combine the Departments of Commerce and Labor because it would be difficult for the Secretary of the new Department to 'tout labor's aims and industry's aims at the same time', Wirtz replied:

> It is as nothing compared with the disadvantages of administering either the Department of Labor or Commerce with everyone in the room, everyone in the country thinking you are a special interest representative when you are not. That is the hardest administrative problem I face in my present position and it is a very real one.[8]

We should not perhaps attach too much importance to the political pressures which operate on a Secretary of Labor because we should not over-estimate the Secretaries themselves. Unlike Secretaries of Agriculture or Defence, their tenure of office is short. Indeed, there have been six Secretaries in the last ten years. Some Secretaries do have a clear idea of what they are trying to achieve. Thus John Dunlop set out to tighten the rules governing union pension funds and to tidy up legislation governing industrial relations in the construction industries. More commonly, like Peter Brennan, Labor Secretaries have had neither clear objectives nor the time to attain them. Because of this, a clearer impression of the politics of governing labour can be gained from looking at more permanent features of labour politics; first attempts to regulate the relative power of unions and employers, including the operations of the autonomous regulatory commission, the National Labor Relations Board, then at a new agency responsible for safety at work and finally at the bureau within the Labor Department, the Bureau of Labor Management Services which is charged with regulating the internal affairs of unions.

REGULATING UNION POWER

As we noted earlier, labour legislation in the United States began to limit union power only with the Taft-Hartley Act in 1947. Scholars are divided about how far the failure of unions in the United States to attain the level of membership common in Britain, Germany and Scandinavia, can be attributed to this Act. It is certainly the case that fears common when the Act was passed that existing unions would be destroyed were greatly exaggerated. However, certain provisions of the Act clearly make the extension of unions to plants where they had not previously existed more difficult. Section 14(b) of the Act allows states to adopt laws prohibiting the closed shop or, as they are often called, 'right to work laws'. Nineteen states at present avail themselves of the opportunity provided by Section 14(b). In these states, all of which are in the South or rural midwest, unions are powerless to prevent 'free loaders' benefiting from higher wages or better conditions secured by the union while not paying dues or obeying strike calls. Many of these states, particularly in the South, have been centres of industrial growth; indeed, industries such as textiles have moved to the South to escape the union shops common in the North. The Taft-Hartley prohibition on secondary boycotts has also made more difficult the organising of new plants or industries. The 'sympathy' strike or boycott is an obvious technique which existing unions can use to help the unorganised in a conflict with an employer opposed to the formation of a union. The difficulties which textile workers are having in forcing the giant J. P. Stevens to recognise their union would be much reduced if it were legal for retail workers in shops to refuse to handle garments made by that firm. Similarly, Caesar Chavez succeeded in organising the lettuce and grape pickers only because he could use a secondary boycott for the highly ironical reason that rural interests in Congress had secured the insertion of a clause excluding agricultural workers from the provisions of the National Labor Relations Act lest they might benefit from its 'pro labor' sections.

The prohibition of the secondary boycott and the 'right to work' laws enacted under 14(b), much more than the more famous 80-day cooling-off period, have constituted an important restraint on the development and power of unions in the United States. Not surprisingly, therefore, these laws are highly politically contentious. It is no coincidence that the Act embodying these provisions was passed by a Republican Congress and that the veto by the Democratic President Truman was overridden by a coalition of the Republicans and conservative Southern Democrats. Southern Democrats since have been keen to defend Section 14(b) as a way to weaken unions in their states and thus make their states attractive to employers. It is probably no coincidence that the fervently anti-union firm, J. P. Stevens, is located in North Carolina, one of whose Senators, Sam Ervin, spent much time watching the NLRB for hints of pro-union attitudes.

States Adopting 'Right to Work' Laws under Section 14(b)

Iowa	Wyoming	Nevada
Kansas	Arizona	Texas
Nebraska	South Dakota	North Dakota
Alabama	Florida	Virgina
Tennesse	Utah	Georgia
South Carolina	Mississippi	Arkansas
North Carolina		

(9 Midwestern or South Western; 10 Southern)

Quite naturally, the unions have attempted to repeal Section 14(b) only when there has been a clear liberal Democratic majority in Congress. It is interesting to note that no serious attempt has ever been started to repeal the ban on the use of secondary boycotts. Indeed, it is a mark of the weakness of labour unions on issues to do with industrial relations that on only one occasion has Congress actually gone as far as to vote on the proposal to repeal Section 14(b). That attempt, in 1965, revealed the highly partisan nature of the issue.

Repeal of Section 14(b) had been promised by President Johnson during and after the 1964 election campaign. Introduction of the relevant legislation was delayed until late in 1965 so that it would not impede passage of Great Society legislation or disrupt the coalition Johnson had so successfully created behind his other proposals. The AFL-CIO leadership and lobbyists, to whom such measures were of course highly desirable, by and large agreed with this strategy. Once the measure was introduced, the Administration and party leaders in Congress hit upon the idea of cementing party unity by associating the vote on 14(b) with that on a wheat subsidy measure which, owing to the vagaries of agricultural subsidy politics, was urgently needed by the

TABLE 6.1: *Vote on Repeal of Section 14(b), House of Representatives, 1965*

	Yes	No
Republicans	21	117
Northern Democrats	182	8
Southern Democrats	18	78
All Democrats	200	86

Source: Congressional Quarterly Almanac, 1965, p. 818 and ff.

Midwestern Democrats. Thus the vote on 14(b) reflected log-rolling as well as basic attitudes. The deal involved not only the Democratic Party but the remnants of Midwestern liberal Republicanism, which supplied four valuable votes.

The 'trade' arranged on the issue held up well.

TABLE 6.2: *Vote by party and region on 14(b) and farm subsides, House of Representatives, 1965*

	East	South	Midwest	West
Democrats				
14(b)	77–1	18–78	63–3	42–4
Wheat subsidies	51–23	62–28	55–9	33–8
Republicans				
14(b)	16–23	0–19	4–54	1–21
Wheat subsidies	2–23	4–13	12–41	1–17
	(Yes votes followed by no votes)			

Source: Congressional Quarterly Alamanac, *op. cit.*

The opportunity to apply similar pressure in the Senate by linking the fate of the bill to one dear to Southern hearts (such as bills protecting the sugar industry) was not taken. This, perhaps reflecting the relaxed style of the Mansfield leadership of the Senate, ensured that the bill would remain in deep trouble. The problem which the unions faced in steering repeal through the Senate was that the Republican leader in the Senate, Dirksen, had decided that his Party should launch a filibuster against the bill. At that time filibusters could be overridden only by two-thirds of the Senators present and voting. Dirksen was able to mobilise quickly a force of 26 Senators, of whom 14 were Southern Democrats and one Northern Democrat, Lausche (Ohio), who were ready to keep the filibuster going. In the event, the filibuster itself could not be viewed as

TABLE 6.3: *Senate voting on repeal of 14(b)*

		Yes		No
Republicans		5		26
Northern Democrats	36		5	
Southern Democrats	4		16	
Democrats		40		21
		—		—
	Total	45		47

Source: Congressional Quarterly Almanac, *op. cit.*

the cause of the failure to repeal 14(b). When Mansfield tried to end the filibuster by invoking cloture, his resolution failed 45–47. Thus repeal failed to command even a simple majority in the Senate. Once again, the pattern of overwhelming support for the unions amongst Northern Democrats and a limited number of Republicans was matched by the antagonism of Southern Democrats and the overwhelming majority of Republicans.

The five Northern Democratic Senators to vote against cloture were Monroney (Oklahoma), McGovern (South Dakota), Lausche (Ohio), Hayden (Arizona) and Bible (Nevada). All of these Senators except Lausche and Monroney came from states which have 'right to work' laws and have a strong conservative tradition, though there were examples of other senators from such states voting for repeal. As the unions were short of 17 votes in order to secure cloture, too much of the blame or credit cannot be attached to these five. The ranks of those voting to end a filibuster usually include some who are against the measure in question but are anxious to move on to another issue; one can only conclude that the measure had no chance. After the vote Mansfield commented, 'I no longer find myself looking through a glass darkly. The image is clear. The Senate does not wish to take up 14(b) at this time.'[9]

The liberal losses in the 1966 elections took the issue even more firmly off the agenda. Only after the 1974 Democratic landslide did the possibility of repeal arise again. Even so two factors made it unlikely that the unions could secure repeal. The first was the certainty of a veto by President Ford. By and large, that Congress was very unsuccessful in overriding Presidential vetoes, and an override on 14(b) was particularly unlikely given Southern Democratic defections. A second reason, however, is that the unions, even allowing for the balance of opinion against them in Congress, cannot be said to have made a major effort to secure repeal of Section 14(b) or other parts of the NLRA unpopular with them. One cynical explanation is that unions do not care very much about the unorganised (though this is to ignore the threat which the unorganised pose to unions). Much more important is that it is notoriously difficult to enforce laws which outlaw the closed shop. Indeed, the administration of the NLRA in general has not proved nearly as irksome as the unions had feared. In order to see why, we shall now examine the major regulator of union power, namely the National Labor Relations Board.

THE NLRB

The NLRB belongs to a genus of agency which is unique to the United States and constitutionally difficult to classify. It is a regulatory commission. As such, it hovers uneasily between the different branches of government, being open to congressional influence through the appropriations system or changes to the law it interprets, executive influence through Presidential nomination of the members of the Board, and judicial review of the legality and constitutionality of its relations. In view of the political disputes about labour law in the United States, it is not surprising that the Board has excited much controversy. Allegations are common that the Board is either too lenient with the unions or too hostile, and deviates from the law. Such controversy is inevitable given that the Board not only operates in a controversial area, but one in which precision is impossible.

Two examples illustrate the difficulty of achieving precision in the interpretation of labour law. The first concerns the imposition of discipline by unions on their members. Section 8(b)(1)(A) of the NLRA forbids a union to restrain or coerce employees in their right to join *or assist* a labour organisation *or to refrain from doing so*. (Emphasis added). Yet the Act gives unions the right to prescribe its own rules 'with respect to the acquisition or retention of membership'. Can a union fine members who refuse to assist the cause by participating in a strike? The NLRB has ruled in fact that the second provision means that the unions can in fact do so. It is easy to see, however, that the opposite interpretation could be sustained. The second example concerns secondary boycotts. Under this section, it would be illegal for a union in dispute with an employer who canned food to organise a boycott amongst employees or customers of a supermarket owned by a separate company. Yet clearly picketing defined in the traditional sense of seeking to persuade peacefully by speech or banners might be protected by the Bill of Rights. The NLRB has felt compelled to accept a situation in which pickets stand outside a supermarket with placards saying that 'Company X (a supplier) Does Not Have A Contract' (i.e., is in dispute with its employees). The NLRB believes that such action is constitutionally protected communication of information or opinion. It has, therefore, permitted what to many (if not the advocates of mob picketing at Saltley Coal Depot or Grunwick laboratories) would seem to be picketing in furtherance of a secondary boycott.

Both decisions aroused considerable controversy. Senator Griffin (R., Michigan), co-author of the 1959 Landrum-Griffin Act, voiced conservative suspicions by quoting one commentator. 'It (the NLRB) behaves like a Department of the AFL-CIO and is about as neutral as George Meany.'[10] Yet allegations of bias come from both sides. The truth is that politics is built into the NLRB not only by the nature of the Board's work but by its own structure. The NLRB is a two-headed body. On one side is the General Counsel who presents allegations of unfair labour practices to the Board. Backed up by 47 field offices, the General Counsel is very influential as no appeal to the Board can be made except through him. No individual, company or union has direct access to the Board. In fact, the General Counsel tries to act as judicially and impartially as possible. Yet the Board itself is not so immune from politics. Its five members are appointed for a relatively short term of five years each so that as they retire on a staggered basis the President has substantial opportunity to reshape the Board as he wishes. Presidents have used this power regularly. Professor Peck summarised the general consensus when he said that

A review of the events since 1954 can leave us with no doubt that appointments to the Board made by Presidents have produced changes in the policies of the NLRB which we must attribute to political factors affecting the appointments.[11]

Professor Winter argues that the short terms served by members of the Board itself suggests that Congress intended to make the NLRB more open to political pressures than most regulatory agencies.[12]

By and large, scholars have discovered an unsurprising tendency for Board members appointed by Democrats to favour unions and those by Republicans business. F. Ray Marshall, in his study of labour in the South, written before he became Secretary of Labor, gave four examples of how the 'Democratic' NLRB appointed by Kennedy and Johnson, helped unions in their attempts to organise in the South.[13] First, the NLRB speeded up the hearing of cases so that the workers concerned did not drift away while their allegations of unfair dismissal were being heard and they were out of work. Second, the NLRB tended to define bargaining units in such a way that in practice unions were more likely to win referenda on their right to represent the workers therein. Third, the Board was tougher than the Board appointed by Eisenhower in defining impermissible anti-union statements or pressures by employers. Finally, and conversely, the Board was more permissive in its attitude to what sort of picketing unions could engage in while organising a plant.

So political are Board appointments that it is very rare for a member to be re-appointed by a President of a different party. All Presidents have maintained at least a 3–2 majority for their 'party' on the Board, Republicans securing a pro-business and Democrats a pro-labour majority. Frank McCulloch, a former chairman of a 'Democratic' NLRB, has summarised the differences in a way which is not too biased but generally supports the views of Marshall.

If the Eisenhower Board can fairly be characterised as generally conservative, non-innovative and pro-management, the Kennedy–Johnson Board might be considered generally liberal, innovative and . . . strongly supportive of employee rights and free collective bargaining.[14]

McCulloch noted that the same trend could be observed during the Nixon Presidency (i.e. for a Republican to appoint pro-management people to the Board) though somewhat attenuated by the President's hopes of detaching labour from the Democratic coalition.

The Nixon NLRB, contrary to labor's worst fears and management's highest hopes, has not engaged in any systematic program to reverse prior Board precedents on a wholesale basis. Nevertheless, the Board has undoubtedly moved in a generally more conservative direction.[15]

CONTRAINSTS UPON THE NLRB

Clearly, then, the NLRB does have the possibility of varying the labour laws in a way which is both observable and politically characterisible. This does not mean that the NLRB is a purely political agency enjoying total discretion. There are, in fact, significant constraints upon the Board's freedom of action. The close watch kept upon the Board by congressional friends of management and unions means that sharp deviations from the generally accepted interpretation of the NLRB or behaviour which is clearly political rather than quasi-judicial, will result in congressional speeches, investigations and even threats to change the law in order to reverse the Board's decisions.[16] The Supreme Court usually tries to avoid sharp clashes with Congress; the NLRB, which is not a constitutionally protected body like the Court, has all the more reason for taking note of congressional opinion.

Another constraint upon the NLRB is the judiciary. At first sight, this may not appear to be the case. The AFL-CIO has pointed out that the NLRB has been sustained in 80 per cent of the cases it has defended before the Supreme Court.[17] In 1975, the Board was upheld in 88 per cent of the cases it defended before the Court of Appeals and 100 per cent in the Supreme Court.[18] These figures could, however, be taken as proof that the Board anticipates the wishes of the Courts or that the Courts pursue a policy of upholding the NLRB whenever possible. Moreover, the NLRB's success rate varies. Thus the pro-management Eisenhower Board was much less successful before the Supreme Court than was its successor, the Kennedy Board. As Senator Ervin was quick to note, that in itself was perhaps proof that the NLRB 'vacillates'. Nor, quite naturally, have the Board's critics been prepared to accept that a Supreme Court decision upholding the Board is proof that the Board's decision is legally irreproachable; both the Board and the Court might be wrong.

It is debatable how far the Courts have intervened in the affairs of the NLRB. Senator Hruska, a critic of Democratic Boards, has argued that:

> The Courts have consistently exhibited a very great deference to the Board as the expert agency . . . Indeed, the question arises whether the Courts may have unduly restricted the proper scope of their review.[19]

McCulloch argued that in fact the Courts were ready to intervene and that as recently as 1968 in *Volkswagenwork v. Federal Maritime Administration* the Supreme Court noted that they should show some deference to administrative agencies; the courts 'are not obliged to stand aside and rubber stamp their affirmance of administrative decisions that they deem inconsistent with a statutory mandate or that frustrate the congressional policy underlying a statute'.

In fact, the Supreme Court's attitude to the NLRB has been neither consistent nor precise. The words quoted by McCulloch are in fact themselves a quotation from an earlier opinion, but in order to appreciate their importance we have to go back to 1956. In that year the Supreme Court made a strong claim that regulatory commissions had an expertise which commanded judicial deference, or at least respect. In *NLRB v. Truck Drivers' Union*, Justice Brennan argued that:

> The ultimate problem is the balancing of the conflicting legitimate interests. The function of striking that balance to effectuate national labor policy is often a difficult and delicate responsibility which

Congress committed primarily to the National Labor Relations Board *subject to limited judicial review*. (emphasis added)

This raised the question of what was limited judicial review. Did it mean that questions of fact were to be determined by the NLRB alone? Could a realistic line be drawn between statutory interpretations and assessment of evidence, or between interpreting statutes and 'effectuating national labor policy'?

In fact, the Supreme Court seemed to conclude reasonably rapidly that the NLRB was not to be exempted from the rising tide of judicial activism which characterised the Warren years. In *NLRB v. Brown* (1964) the Court ruled that 'limited judicial review' was less limited than had been supposed. Speaking for a majority of the Court, Brennan commented:

In reconciling the conflicting interests of labor and management, the Board's determination is to be subjected to 'limited judicial review'. When we used the phrase 'limited judicial review' we did not mean that the balance struck by the Board is immune from judicial examination and reversal in proper cases. Courts are expressly empowered to enforce, modify or set aside in whole or in part the Board's orders, except that the findings of the Board with respect to questions of fact, if supported by substantial evidence on the record considered as a whole, shall be conclusive.

Brennan then uttered the words quoted in *Volkswagenwork* and then by McCulloch.

Reviewing courts are not obliged to stand aside and rubber stamp their affirmance of administrative decisions that they deem inconsistent with a statutory mandate or that frustrate the congressional policy underlying a statute. . . . Of course, due deference is to be rendered to agency determination of fact so long as there is substantial evidence to be found in the record as a whole. But where, as here, the review is not of a question of fact but of a proper balance to be struck between conflicting interests, 'the deference owed to an expert tribunal cannot be allowed to slip into judicial inertia which results in the unauthorised assumption by an agency of major decisions properly made by Congress.' . . . Courts must, of course, set aside Board decisions which rest on an erroneous legal foundation.

This decision seems to mark a change of policy so radical that it is hard to reconcile with *NLRB v. Truck Drivers*. Brennan 'of course' claims the right for the courts to interpret the law. More surprisingly, he claims for the courts, not the NLRB, the right to determine conflicting interests. Admittedly, this is done in the name of defending the rights of Congress, but the ambiguity of the Act leaves the courts, in practice, much scope to maneouvre. Finally, and leaving the NLRB almost no autonomy, Brennan concedes that the NLRB has the right to determine the facts, but only if its determination is supported by the record, considered (presumably by the courts) as a whole. It was left to Justice Byron White to be the sole dissenter, even though he had a plausible precedent to support his views; he argued that the NLRB's decision should be treated deferentially.

A statute expressive of such large public policy as that on which the National Labor Relations Board is based must be broadly phrased and necessarily carries with it the task of administrative application.

argued White, quoting *Phelps Dodge Corporation v. Labor Board*.

As a matter of legal doctrine, therefore, McCulloch was correct to argue that the Courts are willing to interfere with the decisions of the NLRB. Senator Hruska's view that the Courts defer to the opinions of administrative agencies seems somewhat out of date. This is not to argue that the NLRB does not count. Its decisions will usually be final; the judicial system is sufficiently busy already to avoid reviewing every labour case. Some idea of the relative frequency of judicial intervention can be gathered from Table 6.4.

TABLE 6.4: *NLRB work load in Fiscal Year 1975*

	Number of Cases
Allegations of unfair labour practices closed	29,808
Employee representation cases closed	13,899
Total of cases closed (all types)	43,707
Total contested Board decisions	1,415

Source: NLRB *Annual Report*, 1975

As can be seen, most of the cases taken up by the NLRB are settled, often by field or regional offices with no reference to Washington. However, of the cases that do reach the Board, only a minority reach the Courts of Appeal or Supreme Court (see Table 6.5).

TABLE 6.5:   *The NLRB in the Courts of Appeal*
(Fiscal Year 1975)

Result	Number of cases
Affirmed in full	189
Affirmed with modification	21
Remanded to NLRB	8
Partially affirmed and partially remanded	11
Set aside	32
Total NLRB cases ruled on	261

Source: NLRB *Annual Report*, 1975

In the same year the Supreme Court affirmed in full six NLRB decisions and affirmed one with modification. The NLRB appeared as *amicus curiae* (entering an advisory brief) in two cases but in neither was the Board's position adopted.

Thus the NLRB is in practice the institution which settles most disputes conducted within the National Labor Relations Act. The upshot of the current position of the Supreme Court on the autonomy of the Board is that the NLRB still matters a great deal to unions in practice, but that on issues of major principle, the composition of the courts, and the Supreme Court in particular, is also of great significance. Thus, self-interest compels American unions to take an interest in politics, for the attitude of the President reflected in the sort of person he appoints to the NLRB or Supreme Court will affect the ability of unions to pursue their industrial objectives successfully. The election of a president who will nominate sympathetic people to the Board and the courts, and the election of sympathetic senators to confirm the nominations is vital to the unions' self-interest. The extensive nature of the system of labour law in the United States compels unions to think politically.

It is not perhaps logically necessary that a Supreme Court which is liberal on race or civil liberties should be sympathetic to labour unions. In practice, however, the two have gone together. Thus, of the nominees that President Nixon put forward for a place on the Supreme Court in order to appeal to the South, Haynsworth and Carswell, Haynsworth had a clear record of anti-union as well as anti-black judgments. Viewed more positively, the Warren Court whose major record was, of course, created in the field of civil rights and liberties, also tended to be sympathetic to the unions. It is significant that one of the worst periods for the NLRB in terms of being overruled by the Court was when it was dominated by pro-business Eisenhower appointees; in that period pro-NLRB rulings were reversed by the Court on five major issues. Similarly, the 'Nixon' or 'Burger' Court has shown a tendency to find against the unions. Thus the imposition of a minimum wage on state and local governments was deemed unconstitutional, this being a major blow to the public service unions. The desire or need for a more sympathetic Supreme Court was a major factor in lining the unions up behind the Democratic Party's nominee in 1976.

It has been commonplace to record the importance of such locally elected officials as judges, sheriffs and safety commissioners. The attitude which local law enforcement officers take towards a picket, for example, can be crucial to the success or failure of a strike. It is at least as, and probably more, important however, to record the significance of the ways in which the Supreme Court and NLRB interpret the labour laws. Both bodies exercise immense discretion which can affect the balance of power between employer and employee to a significant degree. The way in which that discretion will be used and which side benefits, is politically determined.

This is not to argue that the existing labour laws in the United States can ever be entirely to the liking of the unions even if the Supreme Court and NLRB are controlled by Democratic, pro-union nominees. George Meany, for one, believes that the present system is biased towards the employers. Apart from the Section 14(b) provisions under which states can enact 'right to work' laws, and the prohibition of the secondary boycott, procedures for securing the recognition of unions are proving unsatisfactory. The length of time through which a recalcitrant employer can delay implementing an order to reinstate employees or recognise a union by constantly appealing to the courts is immense; the delay can be a crippling burden to a worker sacked for joining a union. Not surprisingly, the AFL-CIO had made a reform of the labour laws a top priority at present, while a liberal Congress and Democratic President coincide. The proposals advanced by the unions are designed to speed up the process for securing recognition at all stages. Firms would be required to help in holding ballots more rapidly, and implementing their decision more promptly. It is worth noting, however, that while the American unions are striving for rather peripheral changes in the labour laws, the British union movement has no legal remedy against an employer (Grunwick) which refuses to accept the recommendation of the official Advisory Conciliation and

Arbitration Service (ACAS). Even existing labour law in the USA would provide a remedy.

AN AGENCY UNDER PRESSURE: OSHA

One of the most interesting conflicts to watch at present in the contentious area of the administration of labour law is that over the Occupational Safety and Health Administration, OSHA. Its troubles, like those of the NLRB, or parts of the Department of Labor, reveal the inadequacy of standard 'clientele' theories to capture the reality of labour law politics.

The Office was established under the Act (which has the same name and initials) of 1970. One might think that safety at work is an uncontroversial objective. In fact, however, probably the only thoroughly safe factory is a deserted factory. As improvements in safety regulations are likely to increase costs and slow down production, the implementation of safety regulations will tend to pit employers' interests against employees. In many industries such as mining, or, perhaps in the future, asbestos, wages will be set at a level which in part is meant to be recompense for the higher probabilities that those following that occupation will be killed or contract often dreadful industrial diseases. There is reason to think, however, that the safety record of industry in the United States is unnecessarily bad. Thus Duane Lockard has pointed out that though coal mining is geologically easier in the United States than in Britain, the death and accident rates are far higher.[20] In fact, in 1968 (which was a typical year), 14,500 Americans were killed and 2,200,000 injured at work.[21] In spite of this, proposals advanced by President Johnson to improve industrial safety were met with hostility and scepticism. An act was not passed until 1970. Though it was claimed that the disputes were about abstract principles concerning the allocation of responsibilities, the real debate was about the vigour with which industrial safety should be pursued. In general, the unions (led by the AFL-CIO) favoured giving the Secretary of Labor the powers to make and to enforce regulations concerning safety at work.[22] Business organisations and Republicans (including President Nixon) argued that two separate boards should be established, one to make rules, the other to enforce them. Unions argued that such boards would be 'captured' by the industries they were supposed to control; business interests argued that giving the Secretary the authority to both make and enforce rules would breach due process. The compromise which prevailed was to give OSHA (which is, as part of the Department of Labor, answerable to the Secretary) the power to make the rules but to leave final hearings on breaches of such rules to an independent board (though OSHA could impose penalties in the first instance).

In spite of the fact that OSHA had started life under a Republican administration, the initial enforcement policy followed was very tough by the standards of regulatory commissions. This was, perhaps, because of the alarming situation which OSHA inspectors discovered. Three-quarters of the establishments inspected in the first year were found to be dangerous. Inspectors felt that there were sufficient grounds to suspect negligence so imposed penalties on 45 per cent of these establishments.

The tough line taken by OSHA produced a predictable response from business groups. Two criticisms were made frequently. The first was that small businessmen could not be expected to read the voluminous detailed regulations published in the *Federal Register*. The second was that inspectors should not be allowed to impose penalties on their first visit to a plant before businessmen had been given the chance to take advice on how to comply with safety regulations. Both arguments had weaknesses. The labour unions pointed out that the admittedly complicated regulations published in the *Federal Register* were merely the legal statements of common sense, and that workers employed in small businesses were probably more in need of OSHA's protection than those in large concerns. The small businessman did not need to read regulations on, for example, the safety requirements for ladders in the *Federal Register*; all he needed to do was to buy a ladder bearing the label, 'Complies with OSHA requirements'. Moreover, ignorance of the law is not usually a good defence.

Nonetheless, Republicans launched a campaign to exempt small businesses and farmers. In 1975, Rep. Paul Findley (Republican, Ill.) moved an amendment to prevent OSHA inspectors from imposing penalties for breaches of safety regulations on their first visit to a factory, a move aimed at weakening the tough enforcement policy OSHA had adopted. Rep. Robert E. Bauman (Republican, Maryland) said that the real issue was

whether you are on the side of a Gestapo which can knock on your door at any time and tell you how to run your business or whether they will put you out of business, or whether, under the free enterprise system, we will provide safe jobs.[23]

In 1975, Findley's amendment was rejected decisively with Republicans voting heavily in favour and Democrats heavily against.

TABLE 6.6:   *Vote on Findley Amendment, 1975*

		Yes		No
Democrats		82		194
Northern Democrats	27		165	
Southern Democrats	55		29	
Republicans		104		37
Total:		186		231

In 1976, however, Republicans were successful in limiting the activities of OSHA. It must be admitted that OSHA did leave itself open to allegations that it concerned itself with trivia. Nonetheless, the way in which Congress, and particularly the House, turned against the agency was hasty and ill-considered. Representative Joe Skubitz (Republican, Kansas) entertained the House by reading it OSHA's leaflets designed to advise functionally illiterate farmworkers of the dangers of accidents arising from cow manure on working surfaces. His performance had the House rocking with laughter from which it desisted in time to pass an amendment exempting farmers employing fewer than ten workers (in practice nearly all farmers) from OSHA regulations. Representative Findley seized his opportunity and added a further amendment to exempt small businessmen too.

Once again, though more sympathetic towards unions than Republicans, even Northern Democrats had proved shaky on a labour issue. In the Senate, however, a determined, though not particularly competent, campaign by Senator James Durkin, fresh from capturing New Hampshire for the Democrats with massive support from the unions, succeeded in restoring a limited degree of control by OSHA over small businesses, though not over farmers, by offering fresh amendments and lobbying hard for them.

It says much for the determination of OSHA's officials that after seven years of attack, they remain keen advocates of effective safety regulations. They have not been 'captured'. It is worth specifying how the pressures on OSHA from the business community were expressed, for they were not from the sources that clientele theory would predict. The first source was, in fact, the Presidency. One of the ways suggested to President Nixon to solicit business contributions for the Committee

TABLE 6.7   *Votes to Exempt from OSHA Regulations*

		Yes		No
1.	Farmers			
	Democrats		148	113
	Northern Democrats	75		105
	Southern Democrats	73		8
	Republicans		125	11
	Total		273	124
2.	Small Businesses			
	Democrats		117	141
	Northern Democrats	50		128
	Southern Democrats	67		13
	Republicans		114	20
	Total		231	161

to Re-Elect the President (CREEP) was to promise businessmen that OSHA would be ordered to 'go easy' in enforcing safety regulations. A second source of pressure came not from the relevant Committees of Congress, as clientele theory would predict, but the ordinary members on the floor who backed the Skubitz and Findley amendments. When it came to the crunch, even the heavily Democratic, liberal Congress, elected in the aftermath of Watergate, lacked the determination to back up an agency pursuing safety vigorously but accused by businessmen of pettiness and interference. So far, OSHA has not been a victim of the pressures associated with clientelism; it has, however, suffered from the lack of support customary in the United States for regulating business strictly.

THE GOVERNMENT AND CORRUPTION

Few aspects of unions in the United States have been as extensively publicised as corruption. This, quite reasonably, not only has caused a reduction in the prestige of the unions concerned, but has also been exploited politically to reduce the industrial power of unions in general against whom no serious allegations have been made. Corruption in American unions takes many forms. In the dock area of New York, the International Longshoremen's Association (ILA) operated a form of racketeering in which strategically placed officials extorted payments from employers all too willing to pay for a docile workforce and prompt loading of ships. The president of the United Mineworkers, Tony Boyle, was prepared to use any method, including murder, to defeat his rivals. Violence, too, has besmirched the internal politics of the Teamsters, the largest and most powerful of the American unions. Moreover, its national leadership has often been linked to the Mafia which, it is alleged, helped national union figures to power in exchange for 'kick-back' payments and loans from the Teamsters' large pension funds which the Mafia used to finance property developments in Florida and Las Vegas.

It is important to emphasise, if only because the press so rarely does, that the American labour movement is not in general corrupt and that the examples quoted refer only to a minority of unions. Nonetheless, such examples are worrying, particularly as the law seems helpless to prevent them. There is something deeply disturbing about the presence of the elaborate, handsome headquarters of the Teamsters only four hundred yards from the Capitol when allegations of corruption inside that union are so common. Indeed, it is equally disturbing that in spite of these allegations, so many well known congressmen and senators of both parties accept campaign contributions from the Teamsters. Why American unions are more corrupt than unions in Europe is beyond the scope of this study. Whether the answer lies in the unions or in the society of which they are part (and in which corruption is rife) can be the subject of endless speculation. While it is worth noting for our purposes that the corrupt unions are also the most conservative politically, our concern here is merely to outline why, in spite of the adequacy of the law, the federal government has not rooted out corruption.

That the law is adequate needs little discussion. The usual provisions of criminal and civil law against violence, intimidation, embezzlement and ballot rigging have been supplemented by special provisions aimed at union corruption. The chief of these were contained in the Landrum-Griffin Act of 1959 amending the NLRA, the Act being known as the Labor Management Reporting and Disclosure Act, LMRDA. The LMRDA contained two crucial sections aimed at the abuse of power within unions. The first of these was a union members' 'Bill of Rights' guaranteeing, as the title suggests, the basic rights of freedom of expression, freedom from unfair dismissal and the right to have fair elections (though not freedom from racial discrimination). Upon receipt of *prima facie* evidence, the Secretary of Labor is empowered to seek court orders securing compliance with the Act. More specifically aimed at the prevention of corruption are the major provisions of the

Act requiring the filing with the Labor Department of reports covering the financial activities of the union. These reports are expected to bring to light criminal practices and to encourage the membership to insist on better behaviour from their officials. A special unit of the Labor Department, originally called the Bureau of Labor Management Reporting, was created to administer these sections of the Act. How, then, is the failure to root out corruption to be explained?

A key, possibly *the* key, to understanding the behaviour of the Bureau, is its feeling of vulnerability. This feeling is traceable to the fact that even honest unions do not like the LMRDA. At the time Landrum-Griffin was passed unions feared the increase in the involvement of government in their affairs further diminishing their power, and resented the passing of legislation aimed at *union* corruption alone rather than corruption in general, covering corruption in business and politics as well. Moreover, the open attempts by Landrum and Griffin to confuse the issues of preventing corruption, on the one hand, and of reducing the power of the unions industrially, on the other, got the Act off to a poor start. The fears of the unions were strengthened when the Bureau hired its staff from the ranks of law enforcement agencies such as the FBI and Internal Revenue Service, thereby indicating that it intended to take a 'tough' approach. Of course, unions with something to hide were particularly unsympathetic but the antagonism of honest unions created two major problems for the Bureau.

The first problem was the Bureau's need to obtain funds from Congress every year. The decisions on the size of the funds to be made available are made predominantly by the Appropriations Sub-committees of the House and Senate covering the Departments of Labor and Health, Education and Welfare. Because of the nature of these Departments' work, the subcommittees attract liberal Democrats sympathetic to the unions. In a real way, the well-being of the Bureau depends on the friends of the unions.

The second problem which the Bureau faces is the degree to which reform can be achieved through the use of criminal law. Given the finite resources which the Bureau has (and which the Appropriations Subcommittees are unlikely to increase sharply) the number of cases which can be taken to the courts is limited. In spite of the help of the Department of Justice in administering the Act, the proportion of all known abuses which can be investigated is small. Of those actually investigated, only a proportion will yield the clear proof necessary to secure convictions. In contrast, the cooperation of the unions will make the Bureau's work easier. Thus, at the most basic level, the Bureau needs to collect a mass of information on union finances, rules and membership. This task is, in practice, made easy by unions collecting the information for the Bureau. Naturally, such cooperation is dependent on the Bureau keeping the goodwill of the unions.

The Bureau has tried to solve both problems by a policy of aiming at securing the friendship and cooperation of the unions. The image which the Bureau projects is one in which its officials are friendly advisers, not 'cops on the beat'. A prosecution or injuction may, the Bureau argues, end one abuse; a campaign of education and persuasion can prevent many others arising. At the same time, congressmen who may object to 'interference' (i.e. strict enforcement) can scarcely object to the Bureau putting on films or lectures about how to run an honest election. As part of this strategy the Bureau has changed its name to 'Bureau of Labor Management Services'. By 1964, Steward concluded, the Bureau was placing 'heavy emphasis on education and voluntary compliance' and that 'the technical assistance programme has been popular with the unions and has helped make the BLMR's relations with Congressional Appropriations Committees unusually smooth.' Only 147 of the 1473 election complaints received in 1963 resulted in any form of legal action, and this pattern has persisted to the present day.[24]

It is hard to see how either the practical or congressional pressures on the Bureau to keep the goodwill of unions can be avoided. There are, however, other pressures on the Bureau which could easily be reduced. The first of these comes from the Landrum-Griffin Act itself; the second from executive politics.

One of the arguments against the Landrum-Griffin Act was always that it constituted a disturbingly detailed interference in the affairs of what are, after all, private, if not voluntary, organisations. Moreover, this interference does not always advance the cause of union reform as the advent of government attacks on corruption against the wishes of honest unions compromised attempts at reform from within the union movement. Thus the AFL-CIO Ethics Committee, active, if not always successful in the 1950s, virtually ceased operations after the passage of Landrum-Griffin; the reform movements in individual unions such as the Papermakers also declined. Though overly pessimistic about the Machinists, Soffer had some justification for the scepticim he expressed in 1964 about the efficacy of Landrum-Griffin. 'The most prominent victims of the LMRDA are the movements for reform.'[25]

Some concessions in the framing of the Act were made to the criticisms of government intervention, concessions which arguably produced the worst of both worlds. The major concession was that an aggrieved union member, one who, for example, has lost a corrupt or dishonest election, is obliged to go through the internal complaints procedure of a union, or attempt to do so for three months, before he can seek redress from the Department of Labor. This requirement has at least two unfortunate consequences. First, any complainant must identify himself, his sources of information and his supporters to committees which, in a corrupt union, are almost certainly dominated by friends of the victor. The complainant thus makes himself vulnerable to political pressures and worse. In the case of the United Mineworkers, the aggrieved reform candidate, Joseph Yablonski, was murdered (along with his family) before he could exhaust the complaint procedures of the UMW.[26] The second defect of the requirement to seek redress within the union is that the issue, if delayed sufficiently, can be moot before it reaches court; the victor of a dishonest election may well have completed his term of office. In fact, in the case of the UMW, the murder of Yablonski prompted the Labor Department to intervene immediately, even though the complaint procedure had yet to be completed within the Union.

Though the Labor Department's refusal to become involved before Yablonski's death was due in part to political pressures which we shall now examine, it was also caused by the unsatisfactory nature of the law itself. A greater willingness on the part of the Department of Labor to intervene in exceptional cases, and clearer legal entitlement to do so, would increase the effectiveness of the drive against corruption and the unscrupulous use of power.

A second, and more controversial, factor is the impact of national party politics. The Democrats are, of course, normally considered to be the party of labour. We have seen earlier how the overwhelming majority of the unions' political endorsements are from the ranks of the Democrats, and that the AFL-CIO's Committee on Political Education has made a major contribution to the election campaign of every Democratic candidate for the Presidency since 1952, except for McGovern. Yet in recent times, the supposed resentment of blue collar workers directed against the liberal Democrats because of criticism of American involvement in Vietnam and tolerance of unconventional life styles at home encouraged the Republicans to try to make inroads into the Democrats' support amongst the unions. Probably not by coincidence, the more right wing unions tend to be the more corrupt; it is possible that the absence of any crusading ideology is one of the factors which makes a union such as the Teamsters more open to criminal influences than, say, the United Auto Workers. A Republican attempt to improve relations with the unions (which, as we have seen, is not without its difficulties) encounters the embarrassing fact that its best chance of success lies with unions which are far from honest.

Examining the impact of party competition and strategy on the administration of justice is not easy, as the history of the Watergate affair shows. Yet there is some evidence to suggest that the Republican administrations, particularly that under Richard Nixon, have compromised on vigorous enforcement of measures designed to combat corruption in exchange for political support. The crudest example of this was the courting of the Teamsters. After a conference with Nixon at the White House, the President of the Teamsters, Frank Fitzsimmons', request that his predecessor, Jimmy Hoffa, be paroled, was granted. He had been imprisoned for tampering with a jury, the result of a major drive by the Justice Department against labour gangsters launched by Robert Kennedy in 1961. The Teamsters then endorsed Nixon for the 1972 election. (Hoffa did not enjoy his liberty for long. When he defied warnings from the Mafia and tried to displace Fitzsimmons and recover the Presidency of the Teamsters, he was murdered.) President Ford's Secretary of Labor, William Usery, continued the courtship. Usery attended the Conference of the Teamsters, itself a dubious move when his Department was actively investigating the union, and then made a speech paying fulsome tribute to the union. Early in his remarks, Usery said: 'Let me assure you that even though I don't have a Teamsters card I belong to this club because I believe in it.' Later he made the extraordinary statement that 'Bringing a better life to all Americans is what it's all about. The International Brotherhood of Teamsters and, yes, the United States Department of Labor . . . share in that goal.'[27] To their credit, Senators such as Durkin (Democrat, New Hampshire) closely linked to the bulk of the labour movement, including the AFL-CIO, protested vigorously about Usery's tasteless remarks.

What effect does such a courtship have on the activities of the Bureau of Labor Management Services? Quite clearly, it inhibits its admittedly weak investigative efforts. This is partly a matter of psychology. As one official of the Bureau put it to me, 'It's difficult to launch an investigation of a union when the President is climbing into bed with it.' More discreet pressure comes through the budgetary process. After the UMW affair, and the massive publicity which followed the murder of the Yablonski family, the number of complaints of malpractice in the affairs of the union made to the Bureau increased sharply. Yet the budget allocated to the Bureau, far from being increased to cope with the extra work, was actually cut. The Republican Secretaries of Labor also transferred personnel from the Bureau to other sections of the Department. One of the Bureau's officials, questioned about the impact of politics on its work, described these pressures and then commented, 'They (politicians) don't give you a direct order, but if you find your budget cut and your staff reduced you get the message.' It is only fair to add that the Office of Management and Budget has followed a general policy of encouraging agencies like the Bureau of Labor Management Services to switch from a strategy of law enforcement to one of education. Yet the misfortunes of the Bureau also reflect the priorities of Republican Presidents trying to secure good relations with conservative unions.

In general, then, the Bureau of Labor Management Services experiences all the problems such as securing appropriations and needing the practical cooperation of the people it regulates which weaken most regulatory bodies in the United States. Its efforts have also been handicapped by a particular concern not to allow the government to become too deeply enmeshed in the affairs of unions, and by the competition between the parties for the loyalty of labour unions, including those of a dubious legal standing.

Ironically, one final factor weakening the impact of the Bureau in combating malpractice has been that when the courts have become interested in the affairs of unions, they have laid down such stringent rules to guide the agency's officials that the Bureau has been stretched to the uttermost. Thus in the affair of the UMW, a federal judge ordered the Bureau to re-run the election. Arnold Miller, who had succeeded Yablonski as the reform candidate, won. The judge also laid down the rules and procedures for the election. The rules were designed to minimise the chances of further malpractice. No miner other than the voter was to touch a ballot paper at any stage. To prevent intimidation by roaming bands of pickets or thugs, the election was to take place in all the union's one thousand districts simultaneously; all the ballots were to be counted by the Bureau in Washington. These requirements stretched the Bureau to the full. The cost of providing poll-watchers and collecting the ballots required more staff than the Bureau had. All its personnel had to be mobilised along with many others from the rest of the Department, and paid massive amounts of overtime. All in all, running the election in the United Mineworkers, which is a comparatively small union with a membership of only 140,000, cost $4.7 million. The Bureau lives in dread of having to conduct an election on similar terms for the Teamsters, which has over two million members. If elections are to be conducted more frequently by the Bureau of

Labor Management Services, they must be conducted on a less stringent basis.

CONCLUSIONS: THE GOVERNMENT AND THE UNIONS

The United States has an extremely developed, extensive system of labour law. More so than in Britain, the Government has an enormous potential significance in terms of affecting the internal affairs of the unions and their power vis-à-vis employers. This is not to argue, as is so often supposed, that the institutions of government which deal with unions, and the Department of Labor in particular, are viewed by the unions as important channels of communication. Unions are far too important as lobbyists and too significant an electoral force to rely on the Secretary of Labor to put their case for them. Indeed, with the increasing sophistication of the political activities of unions and the diminishing importance of Cabinet Secretaries, the labour unions have come to view the Secretary with some disdain.

On the other hand, unions do care about the way the agencies of the federal government interpret the labour laws. By and large, like their British counterparts but with less success, American unions now want to be left alone by the law. Though federal labour law almost certainly helped the CIO make the breakthrough into mass unionism in the United States, the law is now perceived as biased towards employers and as a threat to the power and independence of the unions. The degree to which unions have succeeded in avoiding the legal entanglements they dislike varies. In the realm of legislation attempting to regulate the power of unions and employers, the unions have not prevented the implementation of provisions which they find irksome. The tendency for Republican appointees to the NLRB to interpret the law in a way which favours employers rather than unions is a significant handicap. Quite naturally, employers keep a sharp eye open for developments in NLRB policy which they can exploit. Legislation designed to root out corruption from labour unions has not been enforced so vigorously and effectively. Though there are many reasons why the Bureau of Labor Management Services has been comparatively ineffective, in the last analysis politicians of both parties have had their reasons for tolerating the situation. Democrats well disposed to the bulk of the unions who are honest have not wanted to upset their friends. Republicans, most of whom have been willing to lend significant support to the cause of reducing the power of unions, have not supported in any comparable way determined implementation of the laws against corruption in the unions because the unions most likely to be affected are those most sympathetic to their party.

In short, the fact that the Government is much more involved on paper in the United States in regulating unions than in most countries, does not make the impact of labour law easy to assess. The politics of implementing matters more over the long term than do the politics of legislating. Yet the most important consequence for us of this extensive system of labour law is that, in order to influence the politics of implementation, unions have to be equipped to act politically. It is imperative for American unions to concern themselves with politics which spring not from idealism but from the more durable source of self-interest created by the need to influence those who operate the extensive system of labour legislation.

7 Labour and Foreign Policy

This book has been a study of the role of American unions in domestic politics. It would be unsatisfactory, however, given the importance of the topic in debates between both the AFL-CIO and liberals as well as within the American labour movement itself, to close without discussing the foreign policy attitudes of the unions.

Attitudes towards foreign policy have contributed heavily to the image of American unions as a conservative, political force. Questions such as whether the United States ought to have become involved in the war in Vietnam and detente with the Soviet Union placed liberal politicians in opposition to the leadership of the AFL-CIO for the first time.

As foreign policy debates dominated American politics in the late 1960s, there is no doubt that this breach was extremely serious. The conflict between liberals and labour on foreign policy was, however, contained and managed in a way which in some ways confirmed the resilience of the alliance between liberals and unions rather than shattering it.

THE POLICY OF THE AFL-CIO

There is little doubt that the AFL-CIO has followed an unreservedly 'hawkish' policy in relation to the Soviet Union and communist movements. In 1966, for example, the AFL-CIO Executive Council not only supported President Johnson's commitment of forces to Vietnam, but attacked 'those who would deny our military forces unstinting support [and] are, in effect, aiding the Communist enemy of our country'. Walter Reuther, understandably, saw in the last part of this statement an unnecessary attack on critics of the war who were also friends of labour on domestic legislation and a threat to free discussion of foreign policy. The AFL-CIO has, less vehemently perhaps, supported legislation continuing funding for Radio Free Europe and Radio Liberty (which some on the left consider Cold War propaganda stations) opposed a trade treaty with Romania (partly because of fear of imports) and campaigned (ultimately successfully) against American membership of the International Labour Organisation (ILO). In 1974, Meany himself testified to the Senate Foreign Relations Committee against detente, calling it a 'one-way street in which the Soviet Union maintains all its political objectives which are fundamentally antagonistic to the West, while it acquires from the West the technology it needs to help overcome the disastrous economic consequences of totalitarian economic planning'.[1] The AFL-CIO opposed extending economic concessions to the Soviet Union

> unless certain political concessions are realised by the United States. These include: granting the right of self-determination to the satellite nations and the German people; abolition of the Berlin Wall; annulment of the Brezhnev doctrine; communications across the boundaries of the Russian empire with no interference in Western radio broadcasts, free emigration from the Soviet Union.

Nor has the AFL-CIO confined itself to advocating government policies. The AFL-CIO has intervened directly in foreign affairs too. Twenty per cent of the organisation's budget is allocated for helping, training or influencing foreign trades unions.

The most important of the AFL-CIO's 'training' programmes is directed through the American Institute for Free Labor Development, AIFLD.[2] AIFLD spends $6 million a year; most (90 per cent) of its income comes from the Government. AIFLD imparts a view of industrial relations which, by virtue of the subject, is bound to be controversial. Industrial relations are presented not as a situation in which conflict is endemic but as one in which unions and management can cooperate to mutual advantage. This approach, clearly recognisable as a description of the domestic behaviour of American unions, is controversial when applied to Latin America where radicals allege that there is an irreconcilable conflict of interest between employers and workers. Suspicions that AIFLD serves the interests of employers, not workers, are strengthened by the presence of prominent industrialists on the AIFLD board of management, in spite of the fact that business contributes little to the budget of a programme supposedly run by American unionists to help their Latin American colleagues. Suspicions that AIFLD is an instrument of American foreign policy are deepened further by the high proportion of their time that students on AIFLD courses spend learning about the differences between democracy and totalitarianism rather than industrial relations.

Moreover, both the AFL-CIO and individual unions have a long history of working to help non-communist unions abroad compete with communist rivals. Thus the AFL gave money regularly to help the Force Ouvrière in France compete with the communist-controlled Confédération Général des Travailleurs (CGT). Before Jerry Wurf displaced Arnold Zander as President of the AFSCME, the union spent $100,000 a year on activities in Guyana directed against the Marxist Party of Dr. Jagan. The union was probably reimbursed by the CIA. The United Steel workers (in association with the British union movement) was extensively involved in Trinidad helping extractive workers develop a non-communist union. George Meany was an eager supporter of the intervention by the United States to overthrow Arbenz, a non-communist radical, as President of Guatemala in 1954, and it is probably that the AFL used its influence with union officials it had trained to facilitate that coup.

All of this may seem to demonstrate that the American union movement is a reactionary force in foreign policy, one of the most important areas of American politics. Deeper reflection shows that the problem is more complicated. In the first place, it is important to note that the AFL-CIO's dislike of authoritarian regimes does in fact extend to those of the right too. Thus in the same year Meany testified to the Senate Foreign Relations Committee against detente, the AFL-CIO opposed the granting of foreign aid to Haiti.

> Characterising . . . Duvalier's regime in Haiti as an oppressive dictatorship, AFL-CIO spokesmen pointed to the ongoing arrests by secret police, suppression of freedom of the press and continued oppression of the trade union movement. The AFL-CIO also expressed alarm that, given the governmental oppression of trade unions, US foreign aid dollars were aiding US-based multinational companies in exploiting the low wage workforce in Haiti.[3]

Throughout the 1970s, the AFL-CIO supported efforts to bar the import of chrome from Rhodesia 'in order to comply with the United Nations' embargo against that nation's white supremacist government'. The Congressional votes on the issue were used by COPE in evaluating legislators.

The AFL-CIO sees little difficulty in reconciling its strong anti-communism with its dislike of right-wing regimes. In the opinion of its leaders, regimes of the extreme right and left have much in common; both deny civil rights and standard trades union freedoms. From Meany's perspective, there was little to choose between a Soviet system of gagged, state-controlled unions and the union system created by Franco in Spain. Differences between the two systems are indeed difficult to elucidate unless one is a committed communist. Similarly, the AFL-CIO's criticisms of the ILO have force. The ILO, created by the League of Nations and its most successful specialist agency, was created as a tripartite body in which unions, business and governments had equal representation. Such a structure made sense in the Europe of the 1920s. However, such a structure does not reflect the reality of life in, say, the Soviet Union or third-world countries in which the government controls both unions and firms. The AFL-CIO also objects to the use of the ILO by Soviet and third-world countries as a general forum for advancing their foreign policy objectives, such as isolating Israel. Whether the failings of the ILO might be rectified by reform from within or not was hotly debated in the West, but the existence of a problem was widely accepted by European trade union officials. Perhaps the AFL-CIO was impetuous, but its attitude to the ILO was not unreasonable.

The impetuousness of the AFL-CIO might seem more like vigour to others. Classifying attitudes on foreign policy as liberal or conservative may be less relevant than classifying them as conciliatory or aggressive. It is difficult to argue that such AFL-CIO objectives as abolition of the Berlin Wall or free emigration from the Soviet Union are 'conservative'. Neither would it be sensible to infer (as George Meany might) that liberals who support detente are in fact endorsing the repressive policies of the Soviet Union. In many ways, the debate between the liberals and the labour unions is reminiscent of an old debate in American foreign policy between realist diplomats and the 'utopians' who believe that the United States should not link itself to degenerate regimes in Europe but should instead be an example to the world. Strangely, Liberal advocates of detente appear more in tune with *real politik* than does the AFL-CIO. The loudest voice of organised labour has been moralistic but not clearly 'conservative', for that term is difficult to apply in foreign policy.

THE DIFFERENT VOICES OF LABOUR

As ever, we must remember that American labour is not monolithic. The attitude of George Meany to foreign policy has been stated. However, Meany's attitude does not reflect that of the whole movement. Thus construction unions find it difficult to take a serious interest in any but the most immediate issues. Several unions on the left of the movement do take an interest in the politics of foreign policy but strike a different attitude to Meany's.

Meany's support for US intervention in Guatemala has been mentioned. Condemnation of that policy was expressed widely within the CIO, however, which had yet to merge with the AFL. This less hawkish policy within the CIO continued. It is indeed an eloquent testament to the importance of non-labour issues in American union politics that the breach between the UAW and AFL-CIO was ostensibly over the hawkish position on Vietnam taken by the AFL-CIO's Executive Council and, subsequently, the activities of AIFLD. Similarly, the three members of the AFL-CIO Executive who voted against the recommendation to stay neutral in the 1972 Presidential election and the union presidents who subsequently endorsed McGovern, were either doves or insufficiently hawkish to believe that McGovern's sound domestic policy record should be overlooked. All the unions within the Labor Coalition Clearinghouse in 1976 were, as far as foreign policy remained an issue, doveish too. Thus there was no monolithic labour view on Vietnam; like British unions on the issue of unilateral disarmament, American labour was divided on foreign policy.

The divisions which existed between the unions on foreign policy should caution against universalistic explanations of the attitudes of labour to foreign policy. It is certainly the case that the union debate about foreign policy took place within the mainstream of American opinion. Thus even such liberal critics of the AFL-CIO's hawkish policies as the UAW were not radical, confining themselves to arguing, for example, that greater emphasis should be placed on negotiations with North Vietnam and less on military intervention. Indeed, there were reasons why both former CIO as well as AFL leaders should be anti-communist. AFL leaders such as Meany himself and most leaders of construction unions had grown up in Catholic, ethnic areas in which hatred for communism was instilled by priests. CIO leaders in contrast had learnt their anti-communism in practical struggle with the American Communist Party within the unions. Men such as the Reuther brothers had worked to displace alleged communists from positions of authority, not only within the UAW but within the CIO as a whole. When attempts at reform failed, eleven unions allegedly controlled by the Communist Party were expelled from the CIO. The CIO's Executive took draconian powers to expel unions for advancing the interests of the Communist Party so that actual control by that Party did not need to be proved. Indeed, proof of Communist control was generally established merely by demonstrating that the policies of the unions had shifted in line with Communist Party manoeuvrings, themselves dictated by Moscow. In brief, although some former CIO leaders such as Reuther favoured a less 'hawkish' foreign policy, they had impeccable credentials as anti-communists. Those taking a 'softer' line on foreign policy within the AFL-CIO also included younger leaders of former AFL unions such as the AFSCME or the International Association of Machinists.

Yet the foreign policy of the AFL-CIO reflected very strongly Meany's views. His anti-communism was supplemented by personal loyalty to Johnson and hostility to Reuther. Thus, the withdrawal of the AFL-CIO from the International Confederation of Free Trades Unions (ICFTU) occurred not because of the 'dovish' views of its members on world affairs, nor because of the prominence within it of socialist trades unions, but because the ICFTU merely tabled (rather than rejected) an application from Reuther's UAW for separate membership after the breach with the AFL-CIO.

One reason for the importance of Meany's views in determining foreign policy was that he had the support of a majority on the Executive Council. When the final clash occurred between Meany and Reuther on the Executive Council over Vietnam policy, Reuther could muster only three supporters for his criticisms of the AFL-CIO's hawkish line on Vietnam. As we have noted in chapter 1, however, the membership of the Executive Council is not necessarily a guide to the most powerful figures of the American labour movement. A vociferous minority movement, led by Reuther, should have been able to demand concessions. The reasons why this did not occur are varied.

In the first place, Meany had, as usual, succeeded in placing men loyal to him in key positions. In particular, Meany brought Jay Lovestone, who had worked for him in the AFL, to head AFL-CIO foreign policy activities. Lovestone, as is so often the case, was a violent anti-communist, in part because he had been a communist. Displaced from power within the American Communist Party after he had made the mistake of backing Bukharin against Stalin in 1929, Lovestone took up a career of rooting out communists, at first as an anti-communist Marxist (during a campaign to help David Dubinsky defeat left-wing critics within the ILGWU) but later simply as a foreign policy hawk. Lovestone's operational control of the AFL-CIO's foreign policy (including activities such as AIFLD) guaranteed that the organisation's foreign policy would be extremely hawkish.

Such an approach had been unwelcome to Reuther at least since the early 1950s. (During interviews with the press during a visit to London in 1953, Reuther was much more inclined to try negotiating with the Russians than was Meany.) Yet his efforts to change the foreign policy of the AFL-CIO were half-hearted and inept. All too often, Reuther was easily out-manoeuvred by Meany. Thus when Reuther complained bitterly that the AFL-CIO had been pulled out of the ILO without the approval of the Executive Council, he failed to consolidate a strong position by neglecting to ask for such a meeting, or contacting Meany to indicate his disapproval, or soliciting the support of other union Presidents. It was typical of Reuther that he should simply fail to turn up to the Executive Council meeting which would discuss the UAW's indictment of AFL-CIO policy, in spite of prompting by his allies.[4] Reuther might well have felt that any effort to change AFL-CIO policy was hopeless. Indeed, the efforts made by the Reuther brothers to develop the foreign policy sections of the UAW itself and even the Industrial Union Department, probably indicated that they did not consider reforming the AFL-CIO from within to be a promising strategy. Whatever the reason, Reuther's failure to operate successfully in AFL-CIO politics ensured that there would be no attempt to create a 'dovish' pressure group which would have moderated the umbrella organisation's foreign policy.

The timing of events also reinforced Meany's grip on foreign policy. One reason why Reuther had not contested Meany's grip on foreign policy was that there was little fundamental debate about American foreign policy until the latter half of the late 1960s. Though foreign policy was the *casus belli* of the struggle between Reuther and Meany, culminating in the withdrawal of the UAW, the conflict was more deeply rooted. Indeed, by the time that criticism of American involvement in Vietnam reached its first crescendo with the Tet offensive and the humiliation of Lyndon Johnson in the New Hampshire primary, the UAW, for practical purposes, had left the AFL-CIO. Thus Reuther, the figure best able to stand up to Meany, was a member of the Executive Council during the period from 1955 to 1966 when there was little debate on American foreign policy, not only within that organisation but also within the country at large: he had left by the time the doves had developed the case against American foreign policy to the full. Reuther's departure left Meany even more strongly placed to resist the pressure from unions belonging to both the AFL-CIO and Labor Coalition Clearinghouse for a change in policy. The withdrawal of the UAW occurred before the doves outside the labour movement had reached their maximum strength, but left the doves inside the AFL-CIO critically weakened.

The conflict between American unions on foreign policy is a fascinating reminder of the importance of general issues in American labour politics. It is less certain what the importance of this conflict has been. Left-wing critics of the AFL-CIO contend that its intervention has reduced the impact of radical unions in Europe and (perhaps more plausibly) Latin America. In terms of American politics, however, the question is what impact foreign policy has had on the relationship between the AFL-CIO and its customary liberal allies. There is no doubt that there has been a psychological effect. Liberal politicians, perhaps never committed to unions without reservations, have been encouraged to be more detached and critical. The refusal to endorse Senator McGovern for President in 1972 was due partly to his 'dovish' views, though as we have seen elsewhere, there were other and stronger factors at work. By and large, however, the AFL-CIO has minimised the effect that disagreements on foreign policy have had on its relations with liberals. This has been achieved partly by using very few foreign policy issues which would embarrass liberals to assess congressmen or senators. Indeed, only one such risky question, the funding of the ILO, has been characterised as a 'key vote' by the AFL-CIO. Relations with individual legislators have not been compromised by their 'errors' on foreign policy. Thus famous doves, such as Senators Church, McGovern (in 1974), Javits and Schweiker, have been endorsed and helped by COPE, in spite of their views. The heart of the matter is that foreign policy is not regarded as an issue of overriding importance by labour. The AFL-CIO would not destroy the alliances with legislators on domestic politics which it has created because of disagreements on foreign policy. In that sense, the importance of the topic to this study is limited.

8 Conclusions: The Restricted Success of American Unions

It is clear that American unions have been much misunderstood. The picture which most commentators on American politics present is of a labour movement which has little interest in politics, except to defend a narrow, selfish interest. Even liberals and radicals have come to despair of American unions. No longer are unions portrayed as either the representatives or allies of the underprivileged. Instead, liberals[1] and radicals[2] wistfully deplore the 'co-option' of union leaders and even members into the American elite. Union presidents, enjoying huge salaries, large cars, expense accounts and the other trappings of top jobs, are indifferent to the plight of America's poor and perhaps even their own members' interests. The rank and file, too, have been absorbed peacefully into American society, which panders to their quest for consumer goods and their reactionary political views. Change in the United States, many liberals believe, will not now be carried through, either by the unions or with the support of their members. Labour, it is argued, is a spent force industrially, organising only 21 per cent of the total workforce with no signs of doing better, and is politically irrelevant.

We have seen that many of the views which are outlined above are ill-founded. Unions in the United States most certainly are not politically inactive. Congressmen, senators and their aides bear testimony to the frequency with which they are contacted by skilled lobbyists employed by the unions, and the ALF-CIO in particular. The Presidential elections of 1968 and 1976 have shown that while the machines of the political parties have been disintegrating, the unions have developed an increasingly well organised machine for registering the voters, persuading them of the virtues of the candidates that unions endorse and the desirability of turning out to vote. Contrary to common opinion, there is no sign that the interest of unions in politics is declining. Indeed, the trend is for unions to play a larger and better organised part in politics. Unions had little machinery with which to influence politics until the 1950s; ever since then that machinery has become ever better tuned.

Research, discussed earlier in chapter 5, has shown that beliefs in the conservatism of the American worker which were so fashionable in the late 1960s and early 1970s were misinformed too. The American worker, the evidence shows, is either part of American society, sharing its beliefs and prejudices in much the same manner as the middle classes, or he is more liberal (by a small margin) not only on economic issues but also on social questions such as race relations. The true conservative in the United States, as Hamilton demonstrates, is not the blue collar worker but the upper middle class white Anglo-Saxon Protestant.

Our attitudes to the positions which American unions take on political issues turn on a number of factors. I have suggested in chapter 1 that many of the disparaging remarks about the political role of American unions are rooted in misconceptions of the political role of both European unions and the American labour movement in the 1930s. The narrow focus of American unions is emphasised by making unfavourable comparisons with the supposed radical activism of European unions today or in America in the 1930s. In fact, many European unions are allied to conservative Christian parties, and as one British union leader observed recently,[3] the remainder are pragmatic by nature. However, even if such misinformed comparisons are set aside, it is still possible to be very disparaging about the political goals of American unions. If one is a Marxist or even a radical, the most important fact about American unions is that they, like every other politically significant force in the United States, accept the existing capitalist social order. No American union, no matter how liberal, currently aims at the transformation of society into a socialist state. American unions, particularly the UAW and the AFL-CIO, however, have followed clear reformist policies in politics which have ranged far beyond the self interest of the unions themselves. Some of the issues which concern the bulk of the unions (led by the AFL-CIO) are clearly to the benefit of their members, along with many others in society: National Health Insurance is a prime example. Other causes which the unions have helped significantly, above all civil rights, are not in any recognisable way serving the self interest of unions as organisations or the bulk of their members. In brief, most American unions have been associated with a perfectly respectable reformist political strategy.

So far, our concern has been very much with the unions themselves. Various misunderstandings about the nature, extent and purpose of political action by unions have been challenged. We might also, however, look at the question in a different light. What difference does it make to the American political system or public policy in the United States that unions engage in the forms of political action that they do? What difference would it make if unions in the United States (quite implausibly) ceased to take an interest in politics?

At their simplest, these questions turn on the degree of success that unions have had in politics. Our answer will turn on a paradox. Although American unions have developed large, skilled political machines to engage in both lobbying and electoral action, their success has been limited. The latter part of this statement will probably cause resentment and dismay in American union circles, but can, I believe, be justified.

The limited political achievements of American unions are to be seen at their clearest in the field of industrial relations. We have seen in earlier chapters that American unions, forced to accept the Taft-Hartley Act, which was adopted while they were politically unprepared, have failed to remove the provisions they find the most objectionable, in spite of the increase in their political power. In particular, the unions have been unable to secure repeal of Section 14(b), which empowers states to prohibit the closed shop. Even that most liberal of Congresses, the 89th (1965–6) could not be cajoled to act by the unions and President Johnson combined. More recently (1977), attempts to expand the picketing rights of construction unions ('common situs picketing') have been rejected by a massively Democratic House of Representatives. Unions find themselves working within a framework of industrial relations law which they find unhelpful in its complexity and slow to enforce recognition of unions and reinstatement of dismissed workers.

Few union officials would contest the claim that unions have met with very limited success in changing industrial relations law. Indeed, many complain openly that those labour helps on other issues do not in turn help it on, say, repeal of Taft-Hartley. Most labour political activists would argue that the unions have been much more successful in campaigning for policies of wider or more general importance.

It is harder to assess the success of unions in campaigning for broader, more general issues, if only because, as they would admit, they have been but one element amongst many working for change. It is certainly an indisputable but little remarked fact that the United States has edged towards being a welfare state. Whereas in the 1950s half the federal budget went on defence, in the 1970s the largest single category of expenditure, eclipsing even defence, was that of income maintenance and support.[4] The bulk of the union movement has supported fully the development, confused and piecemeal though they are, of programmes such as social security and welfare, which account for this significant transformation in national priorities. Moreover, a succession of civil rights acts designed to end *de jure* and even *de facto* segregation have been passed with major consequences for American society in general and the South in particular. Again, the unions gave valuable help in securing passage of these acts. By opposing the prohibition of bussing and the appointment of men such as Haynsworth and Carswell to the Supreme Court, the unions supported a judicial structure attacking discrimination.

The shift of resources into income maintenance is important. Yet the United States continues to limp into an imperfect welfare state, one whose high cost is caused partly by the *ad hoc*, piecemeal nature of the legislation adopted. The high cost of the Medicare programme, which provides medical care for old age pensioners, reflects not a massive commitment to improving the health of pensioners, but exploitation by avaricious doctors of loopholes in legislation which the politicians lack the strength or resolve to close. It is significant that the area in which the liberal alliance (which includes the bulk of unions) can claim the greatest success is that of civil rights legislation. Such legislation, though obviously desirable, has been focused on inequalities caused by racial prejudice, not economic disadvantage. Attempts to conquer economic problems such as poverty, regional under-development, and low wages have been made intermittently in the United States. The vigour of such attacks as the War on Poverty has been uncertain, of limited duration and on a much smaller scale than originally envisaged. To take one obvious example of the slowness of progress, the popular cause of creating a National Health Insurance scheme has yet to be carried through to fruition, although it would benefit many Americans other than unpopular minorities such as the poor, has long been supported in opinion polls, and was requested from Congress by President Truman thirty years ago. Increases in the minimum wage have lagged far behind changes in the cost of living and wage rates. In short, though American unions have contributed to campaigns to improve the lot of the average American and his poorer counterpart, success has been limited. In neither campaigns on labour nor on broader issues have the unions been totally successful.

This conclusion is difficult to explain in terms of the argument to date. A general theme of this study has been the high degree of skill and level of activity exhibited by labour lobbyists and electoral activists. It is true that this skill has not been displayed on all occasions. Thus the passage of Landrum-Griffin in 1959 and the failure to secure common 'situs' picketing in 1977 were accompanied by failures to deploy the political resources of unions to the full. In general, however, congressmen, senators and their aides paid tribute to the competence of labour lobbyists. The limited success of American unions in politics seems unlikely to be due to the incompetence of their officials.

The real explanation lies in the nature of pressure group politics in the United States, the character of American unions and American attitudes to labour.

It is now accepted that American interest groups do not hold a tyrannical sway over politicians as was once supposed. Writers on interest groups have pointed out that interest groups cannot deliver their members' votes as a bloc, that threats by lobbyists are usually counter-productive and that a politician frequently has a choice as to which interest group he will work with. All these points are applicable to labour. Though COPE and individual unions have a noticeable effect in raising the proportion of their members who vote for candidates they endorse, unions do not deliver a bloc vote. In spite of the sophisticated electoral machine and money available to help candidates endorsed by labour, the lobbyists employed by the AFL-CIO invariably rely on persuasion, a sound knowledge of the issues, and good tactics rather than coercion. There are numerous groups such as the AMA and – an increasingly common phenomenon – business political action committees which will aid any enemy of labour. Though American unions constitute a much larger and more sophisticated group than most, they are still subject to the limitations on the power of all pressure groups.

There are, in addition, aspects of American unions which limit their political influence. The first of these is that American unions organise only 28.5 per cent of the non-agricultural workforce compared with 54 per cent in Britain, 68.5 per cent in Austria and 65.6 per cent in Sweden. The failure to organise as many workers as do most European unions has obvious political consequences. Fewer members means less subscription income, which, is turn, imposes limits on the amount that unions can spend on politics. Much more important than this, however, is that union membership is geographically concentrated. In Eastern states such as Pennsylvania, the proportion of members organised is very similar to that in Britain: in the South, union members are very thin on the ground, and consequently Southern politicians have had little electoral reason to concern themselves with what unions think.

Exactly why American unions have yet to attain the membership targets commonly reached in Europe is problematic. I have noted elsewhere that there is a general tendency for membership of economic interest groups to be lower in the United States than in most European countries.[5] Not only unions but business and farmers' organisations in the United States attract a lower percentage of potential members than is the case in Britain. American unions have had to contend with greater hostility from employers and (prior to 1932) the state than British unions. Current labour law, particularly the prohibition of the secondary boycott and the right of states to prohibit the closed shop under Section 14(b) of Taft-Hartley make the task of the union organiser more difficult. The particularly high degree of antipathy towards unions in the South has made the task of breaking into that region particularly difficult, while the existence of regions with law unionisation such as the South has provided havens to which corporations can flee to escape effective unionism has been an important constraint upon unions in the East, North and West.[6]

Yet whatever the difficulties, most commentators would attribute part of the blame for the limited growth of unions to the unions themselves. The effort put into organising the unorganised has been meagre with the limited exception of the aid given Caesar Chavez and the United Farm Workers. The last general attempt to unionise the South was 'Operation Dixie' in the 1940s which floundered, after limited success, on the rocks of union rivalry and selfishness. (Many unions failed to pay the levy expected of them; most cared only about increasing their own size.)[7] More serious for the reputation of the unions than the failure to break into the South was the tendency for the proportion of the workforce they organised outside the South to drop. The cause of this alarming trend, not halted until the later half of the 1960s, was not, as was often claimed, that the United States had become a 'white collar', middle class society in the sense that the proportion of professionals and executives had risen sharply. It was rather that the proportion of the working class employed in traditional, factory floor jobs which the unions had learnt how to organise, was falling, while the numbers in the public sector, routine clerical and service industries, increased. The highly paid, self-satisfied men, often with little flair, who headed the non-political sections of unions, adapted to these changes painfully slowly. Younger, more vigorous leaders, such as Jerry Wurf of the American Federation of State, County and Municipal Employees (AFSCME), were to show that the trends in the nature of employment were not necessarily incompatible with strong unionism. The fact that Wurf was an exceptional leader (who himself came to power only after displacing a more lethargic President of AFSCME) meant that unions were recognising the new opportunities late, if at all. The failure to expand membership had political costs; the tendency for the proportion organised to decline in the 1950s was a major blow to the prestige of the unions. In intellectual and even political circles it became fashionable to present labour as a spent force.

The precipitate decline in the popularity of unions amongst intellectuals which occurred after the Second World War can be blamed partly on the intellectuals. Too often, men such as C. Wright Mills or Marcuse had no knowledge of what labour was like, or had been like, but none the less condemned it for failing to conform to their stereotypes. Yet some unions too did little to boost the reputations of the movement. The International Longshoremen's Association was a scandal: the Teamsters Union is reputed to remain one. It is too readily forgotten that George Meany made genuine, if unsuccessful, attempts to tackle the problem of union corruption in the 1950s. One could add that the success enjoyed by the federal government itself in dealing with corruption has been limited, or that for every corrupt union official there is at least one corrupt businessman and, indeed, politician. After all, most forms of union corruption can take place only with the encouragement and participation of businessmen. Yet the fact remains that unions *do* have a corrupt minority. Those opposed to unions industrially or, indeed, politically, naturally have seized hold of this stick with which to beat unions in general. The campaigns to limit the powers of unions which culminated in both Taft-Hartley and Landrum-Griffin, relied heavily on confusing the issues of union power and corruption in order to mobilise opinion against the unions.

The dubious reputation that unions have enjoyed – no matter how unfairly it applies to most of them – goes some way to explaining why unions are not, in practice, popular. As Bok and Dunlop show so cogently, Americans are very willing to endorse the rights of workers to form unions and conduct the full range of union activities. Attitudes to unions as they currently exist in practice are, however, distinctly less favourable.[8] Of importance to our concern here is their finding that union leaders are less trusted than church or business leaders, or even politicians. Even without the causes for mistrust which some unions had done so much to provide, however, it must be admitted that it is unlikely that unions would be a popular institution in the United States. Claims that the American political tradition is one in which individualism and a belief in the free market are unquestioned, are usually overstated.[9] They contain enough substance, however, for us to appreciate that the collectivist spirit which must always be strong in unions is unlikely to be popular in the United States. Americans are even less likely than Britons to favour the class loyalty and discipline of, say, the closed shop to the loss of individual liberty and opportunity which the closed shop entails.

It is not surprising to learn that unions are unpopular with conservatives in the United States. Indeed, unions are one of the issues on which Republicans are most cohesive and allied in the 'conservative coalition' with Southern Democrats. Labour unions are one of the issues on which roll call analysts find a majority of Republicans opposing a majority of Democrats. Conversely, most Republicans have shown an eagerness to defend the rights of management. Of course, one could argue that in the United States (as elsewhere) the practical definition of a conservative is based at least in part on attitudes to the power of unions vis-à-vis management. It would be perverse in any country to regard oneself as a conservative and yet argue that unions were insufficiently powerful. In the United States, where conservatism above all means defending a capitalist market system from almost any interference, it would be logically contradictory to be a conservative and not be suspicious of unions. Moreover, as we have seen, unions work with liberals against conservatives on a very wide range of issues extending beyond labour relations. Both in theory and in practice, unions and conservatives are enemies.

It is unfortunate for the unions that though conservatives have been steady opponents, liberals have not been reliable allies. The fault for this lies partly with the unions. Apart from plausible misapprehensions about the extent of corruption from which liberals may suffer, on occasions liberals have been treated in a particularly boorish way by labour leaders. By the stage that McGovern was nominated as the Democratic Party candidate, both liberals and union leaders had compiled a long list of personal grievances and vendettas against each other. Who was to blame is uncertain: no matter how inconsiderately liberals behaved, George Meany showed so much aggressive contempt for young liberals that real but bridgeable differences were exacerbated.

More important, because less readily overcome, are the philosophical differences between labour and many liberals, particularly the generation of 'new liberals' who entered politics in the late 1960s onwards. To a certain extent, liberalism in the United States always has been concerned with individual liberties, not class issues. In practice, however, the liberal concern for the well-being of the individual has been translated into programmes to raise the material standard of living of the poorest through programmes such as the Great Society, the Fair

Deal and much of the New Deal. Yet liberals have always also had a major interest in issues such as civil liberties which do not have a class basis.

There is evidence to suggest that liberals have become more concerned with issues like civil liberties and less concerned with hard 'economic' issues, such as the War on Poverty or National Health Insurance. In the late 1950s, the Americans for Democratic Action used almost exclusively socioeconomic issues such as repealing Section 14(b) of Taft-Hartley, raising the minimum wage and pursuing an expansionist economic policy when it drew up its ratings of congressmen and senators. By the early 1970s, the ADA was concerned much more with issues such as the War Powers Act, congressional reform, campaign financing, women's rights and attacking tax privileges. The grouping of liberals in the House of Representatives, the Democratic Study Group, made a similar shift of priorities.

These were not chance changes in liberal concerns. In place of campaigning for broad programmes which benefited most working Americans materially, liberals became concerned with two classes of issues. The first of these we may label as procedural issues. These included limiting the war powers of the President, improving congressional budgetary procedures, and providing for the federal financing of elections. The second sort of issue was concerned with helping 'targeted social groups'. Two points are significant. The first sort of issue, procedural issues, were not concerns which have been associated exclusively with liberals. Limiting the powers of the President was more a conservative than a liberal cause in the 1950s and the 1960s. Thus in foreign policy, the Bricker Amendment, which limited the treaty making powers of the President, mainly had conservative supporters. The sort of procedural reform which liberals came to back in Congress in the 1970s was aimed not so much at altering the ideological balance of power as at improving the efficiency of Congress. Budget committees, for example, though helping Congress significantly in its attempts to recover powers lost to the Presidency, were also likely to please conservatives by providing a further barrier to government expenditure. Even when liberals turned to helping targeted social groups, their concerns were not exclusively or particularly based on class but on other criteria such as race and sex. No matter how desirable, campaigning to force universities to hire quotas of female professors could not be construed as a class issue. Indeed, even the quotas based on race were of most help to blacks who had already gained some professional training and were already close to enjoying middle class status. The three quarters of the American black population who are poor and undertrained stand to gain little. In brief, the concerns of the new liberal are not as closely linked to deprivations based on class as had been the case during the New Deal, Fair Deal or 1950s.

This is not to suggest that the concerns of the new liberals were unwise or illegitimate. The use and abuse of Presidential powers by Lyndon Johnson in Vietnam and by Richard Nixon on a much wider scale, obviously justified a reappraisal of the traditional liberal fondness for the Presidency and antipathy to Congress, particularly as Congress itself was now the more liberal branch of government. The slippage into the quagmire of Vietnam and the expansion of the war into Laos and Cambodia, even though a majority of the American public had turned against it, argued for a change in the way that American foreign policy was developed and implemented. The investigations into the Watergate burglary disclosed the practice of many other undesirable campaign malpractices. It is easy to see why many liberals developed new concerns.

Apart from the pressure of events, however, other forces were at work. Old style liberalism was on the retreat. Many academics concluded that even the most recent programmes developed by the old liberals, namely the Great Society, were failures. Liberals were accused of 'chucking money at problems', of being spendthrifts. A new wave of politicians emerged, such as President Carter, Governor Brown of California and Governor Dukakis of Massachusetts, whose views on fiscal policy were acceptable to fiscally conservative Republicans. The proportion of the electorate calling themselves liberal fell throughout the 1970s so that the Democratic triumphs in Congress and in the 1976 election obscured a trend for advocates of social reform to lose ground. Issues which had concerned the generation of students at university in the mid-1960s, such as race and poverty, were displaced not only by the issue of American involvement in Vietnam but by conservation of the environment, the defence of the interests of consumers and the political off-shoot of that movement, Common Cause. In spite of the radical ethos which surrounded Common Cause, its finances were dependent on subscriptions from well-off, frequently Republican, families. Quite naturally, though associated with the new liberals, its concerns were with procedural reforms which were ideologically neutral. In brief, the issues with which the liberals of the 1950s had been concerned became unfashionable. The new liberal concerns, no matter how desirable, were not aimed at social ills.

Even though the issues which had concerned liberals became unfashionable, the problems remained. Although government statistics showed that the proportion of people living in poverty had declined, inflation explained much of the apparent progress. As mentioned above, poverty amongst blacks remained, even though wealthier blacks found, their progress aided by quotas, that they lived in a period of near affluence. Moreover, the onset of a brief recession in 1970 followed by the severe recession of 1973 caused by the oil price increases dictated by OPEC, a recession which has not yet ended and which has raised unemployment to the highest postwar levels, has demonstrated that the ordinary working American still has problems which merit political attention. As writers such as Levison[10] have argued, the belief that the blue collar worker in the United States lives in luxury and affluence is ill-founded. Levison argues that:

> The affluent worker who, until recently, was supposed to be typical, constitutes 12 to 15 per cent of the working class, white and black. Eight-five per cent are not 'typical'. The average worker earned $9,500 in 1970, much closer to poverty than to affluence. It is an ironic fact that, while many commentators spoke of the affluent worker with two cars in the garage and a color TV, even today, the majority of blue collar workers have neither.

Allowance should be made too for the fact that blue collar workers are highly prone to industrial injury and unemployment, are unlikely to have generous retirement pensions and live in working class 'suburbs' which are inferior in most respects to middle class suburbs. This is not to argue, of course, that workers in the United States are as poor as those of Britain (let alone the Soviet Union). It is to argue, however, that within American society, workers suffer from inequalities and problems which might legitimately be the concern of social reformers.

The liberals, however, have moved in another direction. American liberalism has never been concerned exclusively or even predominantly with the welfare of the American worker. In recent years, however, liberals have lost interest in those issues which were the most likely to appeal to the white, working class American. This may well be one factor which explains the disappointing performance of candidates associated with the New Left, such as McGovern, better than the illusory 'hawkishness' of the American worker. More important for our purposes, however, is that there has been a slight tendency for labour and liberals to move apart. The ratings of congressmen by COPE are no longer quite as close to the ratings of congressmen by the ADA as they used to be. Whereas the correlation between ADA and COPE ratings was 0.98 (i.e. almost perfect) in 1960, the correlation in 1974 was 0.84, high but not as perfect. It is not that COPE uses foreign policy issues to evaluate congressmen in a way unacceptable to liberals; liberals and labour now have different priorities in domestic policy as well. The current Congress has shown already that it is not only unwilling to pass legislation designed to increase the power of unions (such as common 'situs' picketing), but it has also rejected legislation supported by unions to raise the minimum wage rate for the lowest paid (who are rarely unionised). Clearly, the unions cannot rely on even heavily Democratic, supposedly liberal, Congresses to pass legislation that they back. Unions have never been able to regard liberals as reliable as allies as conservatives are as enemies; however, the reliability of liberals has diminished further, increasing the isolation of unions politically.

This isolation is likely neither to diminish the incentive for unions to engage in politics nor the importance of their doing so from the viewpoint of the political system as a whole. It would seem reasonable to conclude on the basis of postwar experience that one of the most powerful spurs to political action is the danger that politicians will treat them unsympathetically. Indeed, whether the AFL would have made a firm commitment to politics if the Taft-Hartley Act had not been passed is problematic. Equally, the tendency for liberals to back away from broad spending projects designed to help Americans on less than average incomes will make the task of unions in securing their adoption more difficult, but also more important. As senators such as Hubert Humphrey, with his commitment to using the federal government to secure social reform, are replaced by senators such as Gary Hart, who emphasised conservation in his election campaign, the importance of labour upholding the flag for causes such as National Health Insurance will increase. Indeed, labour could play a most important role in American politics precisely because, while not being hostile to all the issues of the new liberals, it has not discarded those of the old liberals.

Not all the signs, however, indicate that labour will fulfil such a role adequately in the immediate future. Though unions such as the UAW or the AFSCME within the AFL-CIO remain committed to a high level of political involvement for political purposes, the Teamsters, the largest union in America, remains relatively uninvolved in politics and a source of acute embarrassment to the movement because of its links with organised crime. The future role of unions in American national politics will depend more than anything, however, on the leadership of the AFL-CIO. At present, the political activities of the organisation are controlled by the triumvirate of George Meany, Andy Biemiller and Al Barkan. Though their services not only to labour but to a wide variety of liberal causes have been impressive, they are now all old; in the case of Meany, very old indeed. Sympathetic congressmen and journalists have begun to suggest that some recent defeats for labour in Congress are attributable to the triumvirate being out of touch and less sure of their tactics than in the past. When, for one reason or another, George Meany ceases to be President of the AFL-CIO, it is probable that he will be succeeded by the Secretary Treasurer, Lane Kirkland. Kirkland is a career official within the AFL-CIO. He is relatively colourless and his status as Meany's protegé makes it difficult to say in which direction he will take the organisation. Most informed sources, however, expect that present policies, with the exception of a strong anti-communist foreign policy, will be continued with less irrascibility than Meany employs. An improvement in personal relations with liberal politicians should be possible, and with that an increased chance of labour's programme being passed by Congress. Organised labour, and the AFL-CIO in particular, has the money, machinery and policies to play a vital role in American politics; with fresh leadership, it may play it more effectively.

AMERICAN LABOUR AND POLITICAL SCIENCE

American labour is now firmly established as a pressure group which, even by the standards of the United States, is unusually politically active on an unusually wide variety of issues. In terms of the orthodox strategies open to pressure groups in the United States, labour is the example *par excellence* of pressure group politics. No other organisation, certainly none of the business organisations, can match the amount of money or the quality of the lobbyists and electoral action personnel available to the AFL-CIO, the UAW and the liberal unions. American labour is the example of the possibilities and limitations inherent in American pressure group politics.

It is in the light of this that the limited success of American labour takes on great importance. On the admission of its own officials, the AFL-CIO can achieve little on its own. Its great successes have been as part of the great coalition which campaigned for civil rights legislation. Its worst defeats have been when it has stood relatively isolated on pure 'labour' issues. This might be thought to be as relatively unsurprising in view of the fact that union members are only 21 per cent of the population. However, most interest groups are minorities. Farmers, defence contractors, beneficiaries of oil depletion allowances are amongst successful special interests which are a much smaller proportion of the population than union members; nor are their political organisations as impressive.

The paradox that labour in the United States is probably the best equipped interest group, while not being particularly successful, requires attention. It can be resolved, however, by reminding ourselves of the importance of the cultural context within which pressure groups operate, often referred to as the 'mobilisation of bias'.[11] No matter how skilful their political operations, certain groups, such as paedophiles, are unlikely to make much progress politically: the culture within which they operate is (quite understandably) too weighted against them. In the earlier part of this chapter, I have argued that unions in the United States are a group which must struggle against the hostility of conservatives and apathy of liberals. To repeat: union leaders, even on economic matters, are less trusted than any other socially prominent leaders. Only in the light of this can we make sense of the limited impact of labour's political machinery.

The paradox that labour should have better but less effective machinery than most interest groups is, however, worth noting. For it points to the fact that the sophistication and level of political activity displayed by an interest group is correlated not positively but negatively with the strength of that interest in society. A comparison of American unions and business interests is instructive. Whereas the unions have always felt a strong incentive to combine in order to defend common interests, businessmen have yet to develop a united organisation with half the political capacity of the AFL-CIO. This is not because businessmen do not have common interests; the level of corporation taxes and industrial relations legislation are obvious examples. Indeed, in countries such as Britain where socialism and a stronger union movement are obvious potential threats to business, than exist in the USA, employers have developed more sophisticated and united pressure groups. In the United States, business has little to fear from politicians and therefore organises little. Labour, much less popular, feels the need to organise more. The contrast is the mark of labour's weakness, however, not the strength.

It would be unsatisfactory to conclude without returning to the comparisons so frequently drawn between European and American unions to the disadvantage of the latter. The reasons why American unions are less successful than European unions in recruiting members and are more often obviously corrupt lie largely outside the scope of this study. The central purpose of the book, however, has been to challenge the notion that unions in the United States are less deeply or generally involved in politics than elsewhere. This belief, at least as far as it rests on an assumption that American unions are inactive or narrowly focused, has now been exorcised, it is hoped. Moreover, if the political involvement of European unions and their socialist commitment are stripped of their pretensions, the contrasts between the political goals of organised labour in the United States and Europe are not so far apart as is usually supposed. With the exception of demands for even more cuts in defence expenditure or further nationalisation, most of the domestic policies advocated at a meeting of the British TUC would find an echo in the AFL-CIO. For the fact remains that in most countries, while the labour movement nowhere makes credible protestations of revolutionary action, it continues to represent that part of the population which is paid to do the most disagreeable jobs in society for wages which rarely exceed those of the professions. Any but the most flawed union is likely to favour policies which will be reformist, seeking greater equality within the confines of its society.

Notes

CHAPTER 1

1. For an account which emphasises the diversity of European unions, see Walter Kendall, *The Labour Movement in Europe* (London: Allen Lane, 1975).
2. Martin Harrison, *Trades Unions and the Labour Party Since 1945* (London, George Allen and Unwin, 1960) provides many examples.
3. For a similar view, see Irving Richter, *Political Purpose in Trade Unions* (London: George Allen & Unwin, 1973).
4. Matthew Josephson, Sidney Hillman, *Statesmen of Labor* (New York: Doubleday and Co., 1952) p. 662.
5. For an interesting account of Gompers' thinking, see Louis S. Reed, *The Labor Philosophy of Samuel Gompers* (New York: Kennikat Press, 1966).
6. *Ibid*, pp. 106 and 117.
7. Herbert S. Parmet, *The Democrats: The Years after FDR* (New York: Macmillan, 1976); Alonzo L. Hanby, *Beyond the New Deal, Harry S. Truman and American Liberalism* (New York and London: Columbia University Press, 1973).
8. For accounts of the merger, see Arthur Goldberg, *Labor United* (New York: McGraw Hill, 1956).
9. F. Ray Marshall, *Labor in the South* (Cambridge, Massachusetts: Wertheim Publications in Industrial Relations, 1967).
10. Philip Taft, *Labor Politics American Style*, California State Federation of Labor (Cambridge, Massachusetts: Harvard University Press, 1968) p. 206. See also Goldberg, *op. cit.*, p. 204.
11. A. H. Raskin, 'AFL-CIO – Confederation or Federation?' in *The Crisis in the American Trade Union Movement*, American Academy of Political and Social Science, 350 (November 1963).
12. William H. Mierryk, *Trade Unions in the Age of Affluence* (New York: Random House, 1962).
13. H. M. Douty, US Department of Labor, quoted Mierryk, *op. cit.*, pp. 132–3.
14. Joseph Goulden, *Meany* (New York: Atheneum Books, 1972) p. 464.
15. *Ibid.*, p. 263.
16. *Ibid.*, p. 203.
17. *Ibid.*, p. 274.
18. *Ibid.*, p. 289.
19. A. H. Raskin, 'Marital Troubles in Labor's House', *New York Times* (9 December 1962).

20. *Ibid.*
21. Speech by Walter Reuther to the Wharten School of Finance and Commerce (25 November 1966). (UAW transcript).
22. President George Meany, *Address* to Office and Professional Employees International Union Convention, Philadelphia (24 June 1968) (official text).
23. Goulden, *Meany, op. cit.*, p. 270.
24. *Ibid.*, p. 286.
25. *Ibid.*, pp. 282–3.
26. For a comprehensive and convenient source, see *Directory of National and International Labor Unions in the United States* 1969 (US Government Printing Office, US Department of Labor, 1970).
27. David Edelstein and Malcolm Warner, *Comparative Union Democracy, Organisation and Opposition in British and American Unions* (London: George Allen and Unwin, 1975).
28. See Louis Hartz, *The Liberal Tradition in America, an Interpretation of American Political Thought since the Revolution* (New York: Harcourt, Brace and World, Inc., 1955); Seymour Martin Lipset, *The First New Nation* (London: Heinemann, 1963).

CHAPTER 2

1. Irving Richter, *Political Purpose in Trade Unions* (London: George Allen and Unwin, 1973), esp. pp. 196–7.
2. *International Herald Tribune* (21 December 1977).
3. *International Herald Tribune* (22 December 1977).
4. *Congressional Record* S3276 (16 March 1971).
5. *Congressional Quarterly Report* (15 July 1975).
6. *Congressional Record* S1660–1662 (17 February 1976).
7. *AFL-CIO News* (13 November 1976).
8. Arthur Kornhauser, Harold Sheppard, Albert Mayer, *When Labor Votes*, A Study of Auto Workers (New York: University Books, 1956).
9. Harold L. Sheppard and Nicholas A. Masters, 'The Political Attitudes and Preferences of Union Members: The Case of the Detroit Auto Workers', *APSR* (1959).
10. 'Labor in Politics: How Unions Elect Their Friends', *Nation's Business* (July 1959).
11. 'The COPE Record through the Years', *The American Federationists*, vol. 82, no. 9 (September 1975).
12. 'COPE's Political Craftmen Build Smooth Organisation', *National Journal* (12 September 1970), pp. 1963–73.
13. *Wall Street Journal* (10 April 1975).
14. AFL-CIO, *Rules Governing Committees on Political Education of State and Local Central Bodies* (26 February 1973).
15. AFL-CIO, *Proceedings of the 10th Constitutional Convention of the AFL-CIO*, Bal Harbor, Fla. (18–23 October 1973).
16. I should like to thank Mr. David Robertson of the University of Essex for his help with the computing on which this section is based.
17. *Evening Star* (Washington, D.C.) (5 May 1955).

18. Terry Catchpole, *How to Cope with COPE*, The Political Operations of Organized Labor (New York: Arlington House, 1968), p. 110.
19. *Nation's Business* (November 1963).
20. Philip Williams and Graham K. Wilson, 'The 1976 Elections and the American Political System', *Political Studies*, 1977.
21. In 1976 the AFL-CIO estimated that it had improved turnout among workers by 20%.
22. Kornhauser, Sheppard and Mayer, *When Labor Votes, op. cit.*
23. Sheppard and Masters, 'The Political Attitudes and Preferences of Union Members', *op. cit.*
24. Norman Blume, 'The Impact of a Labor Union on its Membership in a Local Election', *Western Political Quarterly*, vol. XXIII, no. 1 (March 1970).
25. Lewis Chester, Godfrey Hodgson, Bruce Page, *An American Melodrama* (Harmondsworth: Penguin Books, 1969), esp. 733–8.
26. Frederick H. Nesbitt, 'Endorsing Candidates, A Case History', AFL-CIO *Federationist*, vol. 82, no. 9 (1975), pp. 22–5.
27. Gus Tyler, *The Labor Revolution* (New York: The Viking Press, 1966), p. 198 and following. Mr. Tyler was Assistant President of the ILGWU.
28. John Windmuller, 'The Foreign Policy Conflict in US Labor,' *Political Science Quarterly*, LXXXII, no. 2 (June 1967).
29. For a detailed and vivid account, see Jerry Wurf, 'McGovern', *New Republic*, vol. 167, part 1 (5 August 1972).
30. Paul Wieck, 'Labor and the Democrats', *New Republic*, vol. 168 (30 June 1973).
31. *Ibid.*
32. *Congressional Quarterly Weekly Report*, vol. XXXII, no. 23.
33. For other, rather generous, accounts of the Labor Coalition Clearinghouse, see Ken Bode, 'Six Million Workers Minus George Meany', *New Republic*, vol. 174, no. 4 (31 January 1976); and Ken Bode, 'Carter's Laborers', *New Republic*, vol. 174, no. 18 (1 May 1976).
34. Williams and Wilson, 'The 1976 Elections', *op. cit.*
35. N. Nie, S. Verba, J. Petrocik, *The Changing American Voter* (Cambridge and London: Harvard University Press, 1976).

CHAPTER 3

1. *Free Trade Union News*, vol. 21, no. 4 (April 1966).
2. Arthur Goldberg, *Labor United, op. cit.*, p. 214.
3. Goulden, *Meany, op. cit.*, p. 214.
4. *Evening Star* (Washington, D.C.) (4 May 1966).
5. Goulden, *Meany, op. cit.*, p. 187.
6. Parmett, *The Democrats, The Years After FDR* (New York: Macmillan, 1970).
7. Goulden, *Meany, op. cit.*, p. 187.
8. *Ibid.*, p. 301.
9. J. David Greenstone, *Labor in American Politics* (New York: Vintage Books, 1970).

10. *New York Times* (31 August 1970).
11. Andrew Levison, *The Working Class Majority* (New York: Coward, McCann, Geohegan, 1974); Richard Hamilton *Class and Politics in the United States* (New York and London: John Wiley and Son, 1972).
12. *New York Times* (2 September 1972).
13. Levison, *Working Class Majority, op. cit.*
14. Richard Scammon and Ben Wattenberg, *The Real Majority*, An Extraordinary Examination of the American Electorate (New York: Coward McCann, and Geohegan, 1970).
15. Louis Chester, Godfrey Hodgson, Bruce Page, *An American Melodrama*, The Presidential Campaign of 1968 (Harmondsworth: Penguin, 1970), pp. 432–4.
16. *New York Times* (31 August 1970).
17. Democratic National Committee, *Commission on Party Structure and Delegate Selection*, McGovern–Fraser Commission, 1969–72. Archive in Office of Presidential Libraries, Washington, D.C.
18. Interview, Mark Siegel, Democratic National Committee.
19. Democratic National Committee *McGovern–Fraser Commission* Archive.
20. *New York Times* (15 April 1969).
21. *Ibid.* (31 August 1970).
22. *Ibid.* (21 February 1973).
23. Chester, Hodgson, Page, *An American Melodrama*, pp. 733–8.
24. McGovern's COPE ratings were 73 in 1974, 80 in 1973 and 100 in 1972.
25. Goulden, *Meany, op. cit.*, p. 217.
26. The best account of the meeting is that by Jerry Wurf, President of AFSCME in *New Republic, op. cit.*
27. *New York Times* (11 February 1971).
28. Wurf, *op. cit.*
29. *New York Times* (16 July 1972).
30. David H. McKay and Graham K. Wilson, 'The US Midterm Elections', *Parliamentary Affairs*, vol. XXVIII, no. 2 (1975).
31. *New York Times* (6 December 1974).
32. *Washington Post* (8 December 1974).
33. *Washington Post* (9 December 1974).
34. *Ibid.*
35. *New York Times* (13 December 1974).
36. *Ibid.* (6 December 1974).
37. On the increased importance of caucuses, *vide* Davis G. Sullivan, Jeffrey L. Pressman, F. Christopher Arterton, *Exploration in Convention Decision Making*, (San Francisco: W. H. Freeman and Co., 1976).
38. *New York Times* (6 December 1974).
39. Paul Wieck, *New Republic*, vol. 171, no. 25 (13 December 1974).
40. *New York Times* (6 December 1974).
41. Ken Bode, 'Six Million Workers Minus George Meany', *New Republic*, vol. 174, no. 4 (31 January 1976); 'Carter's Laborers', *New Republic*, vol. 174, no. 18 (1 May 1976).
42. *Congressional Quarterly Weekly Report*, vol XXX, no. 46.
43. *New York Times* (28 September 1976).

44. AFL-CIO News Release (17 May 1972).
45. AFL-CIO Federationist, vol. 83 no. 6 (August 1976).
46. AFL-CIO, *Federationist*, vol 82, no. 9, 1976.
47. Ibid.

CHAPTER 4

1. R. Bauer, I. Poole and A. Dexter, *American Business and Public Policy* (London and New York: Prentice Hall International, 1964); see also Theodore Marmor, *The Politics of Medicare* (London: Library of Social Policy and Administration, Routledge and Kegan Paul, 1970), in which he puts the power of the American Medical Association into context.
2. I am very grateful to the members of Congress, senators and their aides who have given me the interviews on which much of this section is based; naturally, I shall not attribute to them remarks made in private.
3. *Congressional Quarterly Weekly Report*, 'The AFL-CIO: How Much Clout in Congress?' (19 July 1975) pp. 1531—40.
4. Haynes Johnson and Nick Kotz, *Washington Post* (13 April 1972).
5. *Congressional Quarterly Weekly Report*, op. cit., p. 1533.
6. Richard Harris, *A Sacred Trust* (Harmondsworth: Pelican Books, 1969) pp. 200—1.
7. Congressional Quarterly Weekly Report, op. cit., p. 1536. See also Biemiller's own estimate of the importance of local activity in A. Biemiller, "Legislative Activities of Labor," *Issues in Industrial Society*, vol. 1, no. 2, 1969.
8. US Congress, House of Representatives, Committee on Education and Labor, *Hearings on Repeal of Section 14(b) of* the Labor Management Relations Act, 85th Congress, 1st Session, pp. 215, 648—51, 987, 988.
9. *Washington Post* (13 April 1972).
10. *Congressional Quarterly Weekly Report*, op. cit.
11. *Ibid.*, p. 1533.
12. *Ibid.*
13. Alan K. McAdams, *Power and Politics in Labor Legislation* (New York and London: University of Columbia Press, 1964).
14. Goulden, *Meany*, op. cit., p. 298.
15. Interviews.
16. David E. Price, *Who Makes the Laws; Creativity Power in Senate Committees* (Cambridge, Mass.: Schenken Publishing Co., 1972), p. 263.
17. Interviews.
18. United States Congress, Senate Hearings before the Committee on Labor and Public Welfare, 91st Congress, 2nd Session (1972), p. 207 and ff. For Meany's testimony in support of NHI, see p. 267 and ff.
19. *Labor Looks at Congress*, 1973. An AFL-CIO Legislative Report (Washington DC: 1974), p. 111.
20. See, for example, the remarks of Evelyn Dubrow of the ILGWU in *Congressional Quarterly Weekly Report*, op. cit.
21. Interviews.
22. Again, interviews were conducted on the basis of confidentiality.

23. A list of the occasions on which AFL-CIO lobbyists have appeared to support civil rights legislation should include:

US Congress – House of Representatives, Committee on the Judiciary, Hearings before Subcommittee no. 5, 85th Congress, 1st Session (1957) (statement by Biemiller, pp. 646 and ff).

House of Representatives, Committee on the Judiciary, *Civil Rights, 1966*, Hearings before Subcommittee no. 5, 85th Congress 2nd Session, pp. 1607–16.

House of Representatives, Committee on the Judiciary, Hearings before Subcommittee no. 5, 88th Congress, 1st Session.

House of Representatives, Committee on the Judiciary, *Voting Rights*, Hearings before Subcommittee no. 5, 89th Congress, on HR 6400 (statement by Meany, p. 460 and ff).

Senate, Committee on Labor and Public Welfare, Subcommittee on Labor, *Equal Employment Opportunity Act of 1971*, Hearings, 92nd Congress, 1st Session (1972).

House of Representatives, *Equal Employment Opportunity Enforcement Procedures*, Hearings before Subcommittee on Labor of the Committee on Education and Labor, 91st Congress, 1st and 2nd Sessions, p. 100 and ff.

24. US Congress, Senate, *Civil Rights Act of 1967*, Hearings before the Subcommittee on Constitutional Rights, 86th Congress, 2nd Session, p. 307 and f. (Harris) and *Fair Housing Act of 1967*, Hearings before the Subcommittee on Housing and Urban Affairs, Committee on Banking and Currency, 90th Congress, 1st Session, p. 383–96, (statement by Meany).

25. Goulden, *Meany, op. cit.*, p. 320.

26. US Congress, Hearings before Subcommittee, no. 5 of the Committee on the Judiciary, 88th Congress, 1st Session, House of Representatives, pp. 1786–7.

27. *Ibid.*, p. 1765.

28. *Ibid.*, p. 1798.

29. *AFL-CIO News* (9 October 1976). For the financing by the AFL-CIO of the Leadership Conference on Civil Rights, see Terry Catchpole, *Move to Cope with COPE*: The Political Operation of Organized Labor (New York: Arlington House, 1968), p. 333.

30. In 1969, the *Congressional Quarterly* noted in *Congress and the Nation*, 1965–68, that 'The Lawmakers' actions in the fields of civil rights, anti-poverty legislation, education and other social welfare areas under Johnson's energetic and experienced leadership generally followed the unions' long-standing stance on social legislation.' (p. 601).

31. J. David Greenstone, *Labor in American Politics* (New York: Vintage Books, 1969) p. 332–3; *Congressional Quarterly*, Congress and the Nation, 1965–68, p. 601.

32. US Congress, Senate Committee on the Judiciary, 91st Congress, 1st Session, *Nomination of Clement F. Haynsworth to be Associate Justice of the Supreme Court*, p. 163.

33. Richard Harris, *Decision* (New York: Ballantine Books, 1971), pp. 57–8.
34. US Congress, Senate, Committee on the Judiciary, 91st Congress, 2nd Session, *Nomination of George Harold Carswell to be an Associate Justice of the Supreme Court*, p. 234.
35. *The Times* (1 February 1977).
36. D. Bok and J. Dunlop, *Labor and the American Community* (New York: Simon and Schuster, 1970).
37. In interviews with the author.
38. *The Congressional Quarterly Weekly Report*, 1975, *op. cit.* reports that Biemiller worked for the Socialist Party in Wisconsin before his election as a Democrat.
39. US Congress, Committee on Committees.
40. I am grateful to those involved for supplying in interviews accounts of the incident.
41. *Congressional Quarterly Weekly Report*, 1975, *op. cit.*, pp. 1531–40.
42. *Ibid.*
43. Irwin Ross, 'George Meany, Education of an Honest Plumber', in Jack Barbash (ed.) *Unions and Union Leadership* (New York: Harper and Row, 1959).
44. Jack Barbash, *The Practice of Unionism* (New York: Harper and Row, 1956), p. 406.
45. *Labor Looks at Congress*, 1973, An AFL-CIO Legislative Report, Washington DC, 1964, p. 105–6.
46. US Congress, Senate, Committee on Foreign Relations, *Detente*, Hearings, 93rd Congress, 2nd Session, 1974, p. 403.
47. US Congress, House of Representatives, Committee on Ways and Means, 93rd Congress, 1st Session, on HR 6767 *The Trade Reform Act of 1973*, p. 1209.
48. *Ibid.*, p. 849.
49. *Congressional Quarterly Weekly Report*, 1975, *op. cit.*
50. Goulden, *Meany, op. cit.*, p. 337.

CHAPTER 5

1. Derek Bok and John Dunlop, *Labor and the American Community, op. cit.*
2. Kevin Phillips, *The Emerging Republican Majority* (New Rochelle, New York: Arlington House, 1969).
3. Fred Dutton, *Changing Sources of Power* American Politics in the 1970s (New York: McGraw Hill Company, 1971).
4. J. K. Galbraith, *The New Industrial State* (London: Penguin Books, 1967).
5. Andrew Levison, *The Working Class Majority* (New York: Coward, McCahn, Geohegan, 1974), pp. 17–53.
6. Richard Hamilton, *Class and Politics in the United States* (New York and London: John Wiley and Sons, 1972).
7. Howard Reuter, 'Blue Collar Workers and the Future of American Politics', in S. Levitan (ed.) *Blue Collar Workers*, A Symposium on Middle America (New York: McGraw Hill, 1971), esp. p. 108.
8. *Ibid.*, p. 113.

9. Taken from Survey Research Center (SRC) national sample, supplied through the SSRC Survey Archive, University of Essex.
10. *Ibid.*
11. *Ibid.*
12. *Ibid.*
13. *Ibid.*

CHAPTER 6

1. George Meany, *The Federationist*, vol. 84, no. 4 (1977).
2. For a more extended discussion of this argument, see Graham K. Wilson, 'Department Secretaries: Are They Really a President's Natural Enemies?', *British Journal of Political Science* 7, part 3, 1977, pp. 273–99.
3. In this section, and elsewhere in this chapter I am indebted to the kind cooperation of the officials of the Department of Labor, particularly of the Bureau of Labor Management Services, who gave me much time and help.
4. Goulden *Meany, op. cit.*, p. 429.
5. G. William Domhoff, *Who Rules America?* (Englewood Cliffs, N.J.: Prentice Hall, 1967).
6. Dean E. Mann with James on W. Doig, *The Assistant Secretaries* (Washington, D.C.: Brookings Institution, 1965) p. 54.
7. The leading arguments about the importance of the social issue are in Richard M. Scammon and Ben J. Wattenberg, *The Real Majority* (New York: Coward, McCann & Geohegan Inc, 1971).
8. US Congress, House of Representatives, Subcommittee of Committee on Appropriations, 90th Congress, 1st Session, *Department of Labor, Department of Health, Education and Welfare: Appropriations for 1968*, p. 79.
9. *Congressional Quarterly Almanac*, 1965, p. 822.
10. US Congress, Senate, Subcommittee on Separation of Powers, Committee on the Judiciary, 90th Congress, 2nd Session, *Congressional Oversight of Administrative Agencies*, the NLRB, p. 10.
11. *Ibid.*, p. 135.
12. *Ibid.*, p. 920, pp. 924–5.
13. F. Ray Marshall, *Labor in the South, op. cit.*, p. 332.
14. Frank W. McCulloch and Tim Bernstein, *The National Labor Relations Board* (New York: Praeger, 1974), p. 71.
15. *Ibid.*, p. 76.
16. See, for example, US Congress, Senate, Subcommittee on the Separation of Powers, *op. cit.*, p. 321.
17. *Fortieth Annual Report of the National Labor Relations Board*, for the fiscal year ended 30 June 1975 (Washington D.C.: General Printing Office, 1975) pp. 20–1.
18. US Congress, Senate, Subcommittees on the Separation of Powers, *op. cit.*, p. 899.
19. *Ibid.*, p. 771.
20. Duane Lockard, *The Perverted Priorities of American Politics* (Princeton: Princeton University Press, 1973).

21. US Department of Labor, Bureau of Labor-Management Reports, 1968.
22. See *Congressional Quarterly Almanac*, 1970, Washington, D.C., 1971.
23. The quotation and figures are from the *Congressional Quarterly Almanac*.
24. John D. Steward, 'The Bureau of Labor Management Reports', in Martin S. Estey, Philip Taft, Martin Wagner (eds.) *Regulating Union Government* (New York: Harper & Row, 1964), p. 70.
25. Benson Soffer, 'Collective Bargaining and Federal Regulation of Union Government', in Estey, Taft and Wagner, *op.cit.*, p. 100.
26. For a most interesting account of why the Department of Labor did so little to root out corruption in the UMW, see US Congress, Senate, Subcommittee on Labor, *Committee on Labor* and Public Welfare, 91st Congress, 2nd Session, *Investigation of UMW Election*, esp. pp. 338–9.
27. I am grateful to the US Department of Labor for providing an official transcript.

CHAPTER 7

1. United States Congress, Senate, Committee on Foreign Relations, *Détente*, 93rd Congress, 2nd session.
2. For a discussion of AIFLD, see Ronald Radosh, *American Labour and United States Foreign Policy* (New York: Random House, 1969) ch. XIII; John P. Windmuller, 'The Foreign Policy Conflict in American Labour', *op.cit.*, and Jeffrey Harrod, *Trade Union Foreign Policy*, A study of British and American Trade Union Activities in Jamaica (London: Macmillan, 1972).
3. AFL-CIO, *Labour Looks at the 93rd Congress*, an AFL-CIO Legislative Report, Washington, D.C.
4. Windmuller, *op. cit.*

CHAPTER 8

1. Fred Dutton, *Changing Sources of Power*: American Politics in the 1970s (New York: McGraw Hill, 1971).
2. Herbert Marcuse, *One Dimensional Man* (Boston: Beacon Press, 1968) p. 27; C. Wright Mills, *The Power Elite* (New York: Oxford University Press, 1956).
3. Mr. Hugh Scanlon, 1977.
4. Barry Blechman, Edward M. Gramlich, Robert Hartman, *Setting National Priorities* p. 4, The 1976 Budget (Washington D.C.: The Brookings Institution, 1975).
5. Graham K. Wilson, *Special Interests and Policy Making*, Agricultural Policies and Politics in Britain and the United States of America, 1957–70 (London and New York: John Wiley and Sons, 1977); 'Farmers' organisations in Advanced Societies,' in H. Newby (ed.) *Research in Rural Sociology* (London and New York: John Wiley and Sons, 1978); 'Department Secretaries: Are They Really a President's Natural Enemies?' *British Journal of Political Science*, 7 (1978).

6. Robert Blauner, *Alienation and Freedom in American Industry* (Chicago: University of Chicago, 1964).
7. F. Ray Marshall, *Labor in the South, op. cit.*
8. Derek C. Bok and John T. Dunlop, *Labor and the American Community, op. cit.*
9. See Richard Hamilton, *Class and Politics in the United States, op. cit.*
10. Andrew Levison, *op. cit.*
11. The phrase is from E. E. Schattschneider's, *The Semi-Sovereign People* (New York: Holt, Reinhart and Winston, 1960) p. 31. For developments of the argument, see Peter Bachrach and Baratz, The Two Faces of Power, *APSR*, vol LXVII, 1972 and Steven Lukes, *Power, A Radical View* (London: Macmillan, 1974).

Bibliography

AFL-CIO, *The Federationist.*

AFL-CIO, *AFL-CIO News.*

AFL-CIO, *Proceedings of the Tenth Constitutional Convention of the AFL-CIO,* Bal Harbor, Florida, 1973.

AFL-CIO, *Rules Governing Committees on Political Education of State and Local Central Bodies,* February, 1973.

Jack Barbash, *The Practice of Unionism* (New York: Harper and Row, 1956).

Jack Barbash, *Unions and Union Leadership* (New York: Harper and Brothers, 1959).

Al Barkan, 'Political Activities of Labor' in *Issues in Industrial Society,* vol. 1, no. 2 (1969).

Joseph A. Beirne, *New Horizons For American Labor* (Washington D.C.: Public Affairs Press, 1962).

A. Biemiller, 'Legislative Activities of Labor' in *Issues in Industrial Society,* vol. 1, no. 2 (1969).

Richard N. Billings and John Greenya, *Power and the Public Worker* (Washington–New York: Robert B. Lucce Inc., 1974).

Robert Blauner, *Alienation and Freedom, The Factory Worker and His Industry* (Chicago: University of Chicago Press, 1964).

Norman Blume, 'The Impact of a Labour Union on Its Membership in a Local Election,' *Western Political Quarterly,* vol. XXIII, no. 1 (1970).

Ken Bode, 'Six Million Workers Minus George Meany,' *New Republic,* vol. 174, (31 January 1976).

Ken Bode, 'Carter's Laborers', *New Republic,* vol. 174 (1 May 1976).

Derek C. Bok and John T. Dunlop. *Labor and the American Community* (New York: Simon and Schuster, 1970).

Fay Calkins, *The CIO and the Democratic Party* (Chicago: University of Chicago Press, 1952).

Terry Catchpole, *How to Cope with COPE, The Political Operations of Organised Labor* (New York: Arlington House, 1968).

Congressional Quarterly, Congress and the Nation, 1945–64. Weekly Report, 'The AFL-CIO; How Much Clout in Congress?', Congressional Quarterly Weekly Report (19 July 1975), pp. 1531–40.

Democratic National Committee, Commission on Party Structure and Delegate Selection, Archive.

J. David Edelstein and Malcolm Warner, *Comparative Union Democracy Organisation and Democracy in British and American Unions* (London: George Allen and Unwin, 1975).

Martin Estey, Philip Taft, Martin Wagner (eds.), *Regulating Union Government* (New York: Harper and Row, 1964).

Joseph E. Finley, *The Corrupt Kingdom* (New York: Simon and Shuster, 1972).

Philip S. Foner, *Organised Labor and the Black Worker, 1619–1973* (New York: Praeger, 1972).

Walter Galenson and Seymour Martin Lipset (eds.), *Labor and Trades Unionism, An Interdisciplinary Reader* (New York and London: John Wiley and Sons, 1960).

Arthur Goldberg, *Labor United* (New York: McGraw-Hill Co., Inc., 1956).

Joseph Goulden, *Meany* (New York: Atheneum 1972).

J. David Greenstone, *Labor in American Politics* (New York: Alfred Knopf, 1969).

Richard Hamilton, *Class and Politics in the United States* (New York and London: John Wiley).

Richard Harris, *A Sacred Trust* (New York: Pelican Books, 1969).

Richard Harris, *Decision* (New York: Ballantine Books, 1971).

Jeffrey Harrod, *Trade Union Foreign Policy* (London: Macmillan, 1972).

John Holing, 'George Meany and the AFL-CIO', *New Republic*, vol. 173 (1975).

John Hutchinson, 'Labour and Politics in America', *Political Quarterly*, (1962) p. 138.

Ralph and Estelle James, *James Hoffa and the Teamsters* (Princeton, N.J.: Van Nostrand, 1965).

Matthew Josephson, *Sidney Hillman, Statesman of Labor* (New York: Doubleday and Co., 1952).

Max M. Kampleman, 'Labor in Politics', in *Interpreting the Labor Movement*, Industrial Relations Research Association, New York (1952).

Penn Kemble, 'Rediscovering American Labor', *Commentary*, vol. 51, no. 4 (April, 1971).

Walter Kendall, *The Labour Movement in Europe*, (London: Allen Lane, 1975).

Arthur Kornhauser, Harold L. Sheppard, Albert J. Mayer, *When Labor Votes, A Study of Auto Workers* (New York: University Books, 1956).

Robert Lekachman, 'Academic Wisdom and Union Reality', *American Economic Review*, Papers and Proceedings, vol. 62 (1971).

Andrew Levison, *The Working Class Majority* (New York: Coward, McCann, Geohegan, 1974).

Sar A. Levitan (ed.), *Blue Collar Workers, A Symposium on Middle America* (New York: McGraw-Hill Limited, 1971).

Seymour Martin Lipset, Martin A. Trow, James S. Coleman, *Union Democracy, The Internal Politics of the International Typographical Union* (Glencoe, Ill.: Free Press, 1956).

Alan K. McAdams, *Power and Politics in Labour Legislation* (New York and London: University of Columbia Press, 1964).

Frank McCulloch and Tim Bernstein, *The National Labour Relations Board* (New York: Praeger, 1974).

F. Ray Marshall, *Labor in the South* (Cambridge: Harvard University Press, 1967).

Dean E. Mann and Jameson W. Doig, *The Assistant Secretaries* (Washington D.C.: Brookings Institution, 1965).

T. Miernyk, *Unions in an Age of Affluence* (New York: Random House, 1962).

Henry Pelling, *A History of American Labour* (Chicago and London: University of Chicago Press, 1960).

David Price, *Who Makes the Laws? Creativity and Power in Senate Committees* (Cambridge, Mass.: Schenken Publishing Co., 1972).

Ronald Radosh, *American Labor and United States Foreign Policy* (New York: Random House, 1969).

A. H. Raskin, 'The AFL-CIO; A Confederation or Federation?' Annals of the American Academy of Political and Social Science, *The Crisis in the American Trade Union Movement*, vol. 350 (November, 1963).

Louis S. Reed, *The Labor Philosophy of Samuel Gompers* (New York: Kennikat Press, 1966).

Charles M. Rehmus and Doris B. McLaughlin, *Labor and American Policies, A Book of Readings* (Ann Arbor, Mich.: University of Michigan Press, 1967).

B. C. Roberts, *Unions in America, A British View*, Industrial Relations Section (Princeton, N.J.: Princeton University, 1959).

William Serrin, *The Company and the Union* (New York: Alfred Knopf, 1973).

Rose Schneiderman and Lucy Goldthwaite, *All For One* (New York: Paul Eriksson, 1967).

Harold L. Sheppard and Nicholas A. Masters, 'The Political Attitudes and Preferences of Organised Labour; The Case of the Detroit Auto Workers',*American Political Science Review*, vol. LIII (1959).

Ralph Slovenko (ed.), Symposium on the Labor Management Reporting and Disclosure Act of 1959 (Baton Rouge, Louisiana: Claitor's Book Store and Publishers, 1969).

Adolf Sturmthal, (ed.), *White Collar Trade Unions, Contemporary Developments in Industrial Societies* (Urbana, Ill. and London: University of Illinois Press, 1966).

Philip Taft, Labor Politics American Style: *The California State Federation of Labor* (Cambridge, Mass: Harvard University Press, 1968).

Philip Taft, *Rights of Union Members and the Government* (Westport, Conn. and London: Greenwood Press, 1975).

Joseph Tanenhaus, 'Organised Labor's Political Spending; The Law and Its Consequences', *Journal of Politics*, vol. 16, 1954.

Gus Tyler, *The Labor Revolution* (New York: The Viking Press, 1966).

United States Congress, House of Representatives, Committee on Education and Labor, 89th Congress, 1st Session, *Repeal of Section 14(b) of the Labor Management Relations Act.*

United States Congress, House of Representatives, Hearing before the Subcommittee on Housing and Urban Affairs, Committee on Banking and Currency, 90th Congress, 1st Session.

United States Congress, House of Representatives, Hearing before Subcommittee No. 5, Committee on the Judiciary, 85th Congress, 1st Session, 1957.

Ibid., 88th Congress, 1st Session.

Ibid., 1966.

Ibid., 89th Congress on HR 6400.

United States Congress, House of Representatives, Committee on Ways and Means, 93rd Congress, 1st Session, HR67 67, *The Trade Reform Act of 1973.*

United States Congress, Senate Committee on Finance, 87th Congress, 2nd Session, HR 11970, *The Trade Expansion Act.*

United States Senate, Committee on Foreign Relations, 94th Congress, 2nd Session, *Detente.*

United States Congress, Senate, Committee on the Judiciary, 91st Congress, 2nd Session, *Nomination of George Harold Carswell to be Associated Justice of the Supreme Court.*

United States Senate, Committee on Judiciary, 91st Congress, 1st

Session, *Nomination of Clement F. Haynsworth to be Associate Justice of the Supreme Court.*

United States Senate, Subcommittee on Constitutional Rights, Committee on the Judiciary, *Civil Rights Act of 1967, Hearings.*

United States Congress, Senate, Subcommittee on the Separation of Powers, Committee on the Judiciary, 90th Congress, 2nd Session, *Congressional Oversight of Administrative Agencies; The National Labor Relations Board.*

United States Congress, Senate, *Equal Employment Opportunities Act of 1971*, Subcommittee on Labor and Public Welfare, 92nd Congress, 1st Session.

United States Congress, Senate, Committee on Labor and Public Welfare, 91st Congress, 2nd Session, *Investigation of United Mine Workers Election.*

United States Congress, Senate, Subcommittee on Air and Water Pollution, Committee on Public Works, 91st Congress, 2nd Session, *Air Pollution 1970.*

United States, Department of Labor, Labor-Management Services Administration, *Union Elections Under the LMRDA*, 1966–70, B.P.O., Washington DC, 1972.

Vivian Vale, *Labour in American Politics* (London: Routledge and Kegan Paul, 1971).

Paul Wieck, 'Labour and the Democrats', *New Republic*, vol. 168 (30 June 1973).

Paul Wieck, 'Labor's Al Barkan', *New Republic*, vol. 168 (24 March 1973).

B. J. Widdick, *Labor Today* (New York: Houghton Mifflin, 1964).

B. J. Widdick, 'Labor 1975; The Triumph of Business Unionism', *The Nation*, vol. 221, no. 6 (6 September 1975).

John Windmuller, 'The Foreign Policy Conflict in US Labor', *Political Science Quarterly* vol. LXXXII, no. 2 (June 1967).

Jerry Wurf, 'McGovern, *New Republic*, vol. 167 part 1 (5 August 1972).

Index

165